the Bamboo Cradle

Soft breeze whispers psalms...
A bamboo cradle
    Swaying...
In the night, a light

       Hsu Hwa-Peng

the Bamboo Cradle

竹搖籃

a Jewish father's story

by Avraham Schwartzbaum

FELDHEIM PUBLISHERS *Jerusalem / New York*

First published 1988

Copyright © 1988 by Avraham Schwartzbaum and Feldheim Publishers

Edited by Marsi Tabak

Feldheim Publishers Ltd.
POB 6525/Jerusalem, Israel

Philipp Feldheim Inc.
200 Airport Executive Park
Spring Valley, NY 10977

Library of Congress Cataloging in Publication Data

Schwartzbaum, Avraham.
The bamboo cradle / Avraham Schwartzbaum.
p. cm.

ISBN 0-87306-459-3 hardcover edition
ISBN 0-87306-463-1 paperback edition

1. Schwartzbaum, Avraham. 2. Jews–United States–Biography.
3. Jews–United States–Return to Orthodox Judaism.
4. Foundlings–Taiwan–Biography.
5. Proselytes and proselyting, Jewish. I. Title.
E184.J5S377 1988   973'.04924024–dc 19   88-11049

V 10 9 8 7 6 5 4 3 2 1

Printed in Israel

ACKNOWLEDGMENTS

I RECENTLY ATTENDED the *bar mitzvah* of the son of close friends, Dr. and Mrs. Larry Klaristenfeld. Rabbi Avrohom Gurewitz, *shlita*, *rosh yeshivah* of Yeshivas Ner Moshe, spoke at the *seudas mitzvah*. He referred to the positive *mitzvah* commanding every man among us to have a Scroll of the Law for himself. If he writes it with his own hand, "he is greatly to be praised." In the *Gemara* (*Sanhedrin* 21b) Rabbah says: "Even if one's parents have bequeathed to him a Scroll of the Law, he is nevertheless commanded to write one of his own." Since it is forbidden to write the *Sefer* from memory, one must always have another scroll or facsimile from which to copy. "Thus," Rabbi Gurewitz went on, "every child must eventually prepare his own *sefer*, his own 'book of life,' but how fortunate the child is when, as in the case of our *bar mitzvah* boy, he has the example of his parents' text, a life of Torah and *mitzvos* which he can refer to and copy."

As I listened to these words, I thought how aptly they described the Klaristenfelds. I also thought of the many individuals who, like my wife and me, were raised in a non-observant home. They had no "scroll from which to copy," yet with *Hashem*'s help eventually found their way back to a Torah life. What should one say of their parents? I recalled the instances I personally observed of estrangement between newly-observant children and their parents. How unfortunate, how unnecessary.

A Torah scroll requires wooden holding rods called "*atzei chaim*" which support the parchment as it progresses through the yearly cycle of weekly readings. How fortunate my wife and I were to be raised by parents who always provided us with the encouragement, assistance and love which gave us the strength and confidence to begin to write our own *sefer*. We may not have had a complete text to copy but we certainly had the constant support of our own *atzei chaim*. This book and its story would not have been possible without the sacrifices made and sustenance provided by my wife's parents, Frances and Max Shapiro, my mother, Miriam Baumel Schwartzbaum, and my father, David Schwartzbaum, of blessed memory. Our brothers and their families, Sion and Irwin Schwartzbaum and Nancy and Robert Shapiro also deserve our special thanks for their constant help and encouragement.

Hashem has provided many occasions when individuals firmly rooted in Torah have shared with us sentences, paragraphs and sometimes even pages from their own lives. Without their example, their instruction, and their inspiration we could never have even lifted a pen to begin the task of our own transcription. Our deep and sincere appreciation to Mr. and Mrs. Charles Schreiber, of blessed memory, Rabbi and Mrs. Shmuel Friedler, Rabbi and Mrs. Duvid Krause, Rabbi and Mrs. Edward Abramson, Rabbi and Mrs. Elimelech Briks, Rabbi and Mrs. Edward Davis, Rabbi and Mrs. Yankel Kranz, Rabbi and Mrs. Kalman Rosenbaum, Rabbi Shalom Gold, Rabbi Elli Rubin, Moshe Speiser, Earle Tunik, Mordechai Rabinowitz, and Rabbi Arieh Betzalel, principle of Noam Girl's School. Special mention should be made of Rabbi Nosson Geisler, whose scholarship as *maggid* of my *daf yomi shiur* has opened up a new world of Torah learning for me.

A *chavrusa* is more than a friend, more than a teacher. An attachment and bond is forged which transforms and elevates the relationship. What *mazal* to have three such *chavrusos*. My heartfelt gratitude to Gershon Davis, Rabbi Yehoshua Freilich, and Dr. Larry Klaristenfeld.

In transporting a *sefer Torah* from place to place, one must carry it near his heart, avoiding to the greatest extent possible any slight or mark of disrespect. I carry my appreciation and esteem for all the persons I have cited above near to my heart. Any shortcomings or errors in this book stem only from my own inadequacies. May they not slight or mark or reflect badly on others.

Our story begins in a distant land, a part of China from which we traveled so far. As the Prophet wrote: "Behold! These shall come from far; and, lo, these from the north and from the west; and these from the land of Sinim" (Isaiah 49:12). The Chinese and Taiwanese people have a lasting place in our hearts, but there are several individuals who deserve special recognition. Chin-Lan Tsai and Eli Hahn and their families displayed extraordinary warmth and kindness, for which we will be forever grateful. Toyo Chou and Tsao Chen Wang-Hsui have over the years become almost like family to us. Although culturally very different, we have been able to share one another's joys and sorrows and to grow close in the process.

An unexpected benefit of preparing this work has been my association with Yaakov Feldheim and his staff at Feldheim Publishers, notably Rabbi Ben Zion Sobel, Pesh Fischer and Harvey Klineman. Marsi Tabak's assistance has been invaluable. Her professionalism and competence have greatly enhanced the quality of this work.

My deepest gratitude goes to my wife Rochel, who was largely responsible for this book. Her sensitivity, understanding and constant encouragement gave me the impetus and support I needed for this and so many other endeavors.

And finally, I must acknowledge my daughter Devorah who is the source and inspiration for all that appears in the succeeding pages. May *Hashem Yisbarach* grant her wish to build a family that is עוסק בתורה ובמצוות, that is busy with learning Torah and performing *mitzvos*.

DEVORAH'S PREFACE

TO TELL THE TRUTH, I've never written a preface before in my life! But there's a first time for everything, so here goes.

At first, when my father mentioned the idea of his doing a book about us and asked me how I felt about it, I said, "No way!" I mean, I don't need the whole world to know about me and I especially didn't like the idea of everyone reading my diary and knowing my *personal* life!

But when my father explained to me *why* he was writing the book — to help strengthen some people's *emunah*, to give *bitachon* to others, and maybe even to bring some closer to *Yiddishkeit* by showing them how great *Hakadosh Baruch Hu* is and how He helps us in strange, unseen ways — I thought to myself, hey, not wanting this book published is just plain selfish, because it would be for my own personal reasons and feelings. Once I saw my father's point of view, I agreed. So here it is!

The last part *was* written by me, and everything I wrote is true. It's pretty hard being Chinese in a different country — especially Israel, but I've discovered there's a funny side to it!

I'd just like to say that even though I'm Chinese, I feel only Jewish, if that makes sense. Like I wrote in my *bas mitzvah* speech, it wasn't really a decision for me to make because I feel that I've been Jewish my whole life. I can't remember *not* being Jewish! All my friends look upon me as "one of the crowd," not anyone special, and as my friend Eppie puts it — she even forgets that I'm Chinese!

I'd like to thank a few people very close and special to me because they've helped me become the person I am today. The list is very long but if I started thanking everyone that *ever* helped me, this preface would be longer than the actual book itself!

First, a *giant* thank you to all my *great* friends — Yudit Lantzitsky, who, even after she moved to Monsey, has continued to be my very close and good friend overseas; Numie Silver, who always helped me with my problems and still does, even though she's in Gateshead now; Miriam Geisler, who is always there for me, whether to lend a shoulder to cry on or to share things; and last, but not least, my best friend Eppie Toledano Lasry, who's been with me through thick and thin, who's been more sister than friend. Thanks for all the above — and for *everything*! A big *Mazal Tov* on your wedding, and lotsa *hatzlachah* to you and Jamie. Thanks to everyone for always sticking by me!

Next, I'd like to thank Danny Katz — for being my "older brother", for listening to and solving my problems, and for giving me much needed self-confidence!

Also, I'd like to give a big "thanks a million" to the Friedman family — Moishe, Hennie, Zevi, Ruchi, Malkie, Miriam, Pinky and Perol, for being my "home away from home."

As each year has passed my relationship with Bubby and Zaidy Shapiro has grown closer and closer, and I hope it will continue to grow. Although over seven decades and thousands of miles separate us, I feel as close to Bubby Schwartzbaum as though there were no distance at all. I hope I will give much *nachas* to my three wonderful grandparents.

A special thank-you to Rebbetzin Ruchoma Shain for all her loving words of encouragement and advice.

The biggest thanks of all goes to my Mom and Ta, Dovie, Dahveed, Shmulie, and Yudy for being *the greatest* family!

Thank you, Mom and Ta, for always guiding me on the right *derech*, and for always understanding and being there to comfort me. I hope with *Hashem*'s help I can grow up to be the person you raised me to be.

And last, I'd like to give thanks to *Hashem Yisbarach* for giving me such wonderful parents, and ask of Him that, with His help, this book should be a success, and help to bring all of *Klal Yisrael* closer together and bring the *Mashiach*

במהרה בימינו — אמן !

INTRODUCTION

I HAVE OFTEN BEEN asked by people who know about our unusual history, "Why don't you write a book?" After hearing this so many times, I actually began to take them seriously and considered sharing our special story with a wider audience. I started by putting a few thoughts down on paper and found to my astonishment that I was able to reconstruct verbatim conversations of years earlier. Vaguely remembered events suddenly swam into focus and before I knew it, I had a manuscript. *Now*, paradoxically, people ask me, "Why did you write this book?" There are several reasons.

Today more and more Jewish couples are considering adoption, either as an alternative to childlessness or as an act of pure *chessed*. If they have any hesitations about this important step, I hope this book offers encouragement. At the same time, I hope it informs them of some of the halachic considerations which govern the relationship between Jewish parents and their adoptive children, not to mention the myriad benefits that derive therefrom.

I date my formal entrance into the world of Torah observance to the twelfth of *Iyar*, 5736. On that day, after immersion in the *mikveh*, our adopted Chinese daughter became a daughter of the House of Israel. The events leading up to and following that day form the basis of this book. Since I was an adult of thirty-six at the time, I fall into that category of Jewish individuals designated *chozrim be-teshuvah*. This label evokes a complex mix of images and, at one level, this book might also be considered to be an autobiographical exploration of the internal dynamics of a *ba'al teshuvah*.

While every individual member of this group is unique, I believe some of the experiences I write about are shared by others. In particular, my feelings of frustration and anger, first with the non-observant Jewish community and later with aspects of the Orthodox establishment, may be fairly typical. I have tried to describe these feelings honestly, in the sincere hope that readers will reach the same conclusion that I eventually did: that such emotions, while understandable, are not helpful to the individual or to *Klal Yisrael*.

It is written that after Adam and Chavah tasted of the fruit of the Tree of Knowledge, "the eyes of both of them were opened and they realized they were naked" (*Bereishis* 3:7). After I had tasted of Torah, my eyes were opened as if for the first time. Things I had seen before looked different and I knew I was naked. I knew I possessed very little genuine Jewish learning. My intellect was bare. This lack of grounding in authentic Torah knowledge contributed to my lack of self-confidence and occasionally led me to take actions and make statements which were insensitive or inappropriate.

Seeing the light of Torah for the first time blurred my vision; now the Jewish community also appeared to be naked. I saw that parts of the Orthodox establishment did not live up to my new Torah ideals and stood exposed before my eyes. My anger struck a strident note because my disappointment was so keen. In a number of situations, I now recognize, I even demonstrated a serious lack of proper respect for those obviously far better versed in *halachah* than I.

With time I learned that the appropriate response to the realization of personal and communal deficiencies is not to lash out in anger and frustration, but to turn inward and attack the deficiencies in our own selves, to work on improv-

PUAH SHTEINER

FOREVER MY JERUSALEM

a personal account of the siege and surrender

of Jerusalem's Old City in 1948

Forever My Jerusalem *by Puah Shteiner*

THE JEWISH QUARTER of the Old City of Jerusalem was in flames. On May 28, 1948, after a months' long siege, the Quarter was surrendered to the Arab Legion. All the inhabitants — including the author and her family — were taken captive or evacuated. Jerusalem was torn in two, and the sacred Old City, heart of the Land of Israel, was claimed by the enemy.

Forever My Jerusalem is both the story of the Old City and its people, and Puah Shteiner s personal eyewitness account of the epoch. It tells of the terror and turmoil experienced by a seven-year-old child during the difficult period of Israel's War of Independence. For this was a time of great upheaval — of bread lines and water rationing in a starving, besieged city; of fathers turned prisoners of war in enemy Jordan; of a bitter cold winter with no fuel for heating; and of Katamon, the refugee-filled suburb, "haven" for the evacuated women and children of the Old City.

But *Forever My Jerusalem* is also a story of stubborn hope and belief, of destruction and rebirth, of exile and return. Mrs. Shteiner's words are alive with the uniqueness of the Jewish people, their adherence to a Torah existence under the most appalling conditions, and their undying love for Jerusalem.

That love bore fruit. Nineteen long years later, after the Six Day War and the reunification of Jerusalem, the Shteiner family returned home to the newly reconstructed Jewish Quarter, where they live today, along with thousands of other Jews, in a vibrant, flourishing community.

Translated from the Hebrew *Mitoch Hahafeycha* by Bracha Slae. 288 pp. hardcover $14.95   paperback $11.95

Philipp Feldheim Inc.
200 Airport Executive Park, Spring Valley, N.Y. 10977

Feldheim Publishers Ltd.
P.O. Box 6525, Jerusalem, Israel

ing ourselves first, and only then, to work on behalf of the community, in a spirit of *ahavas Yisrael*. This is one of the messages of my book.

My primary motivation in writing this book was to tell the story of a Jewish girl who happens to be Chinese and happens to be my daughter. The way in which Devorah has dealt with, and continues to deal with her special situation serves as an example to all those who, for one reason or another, feel that they are somehow *different*. It was precisely her different-ness that moved us to embark on a voyage more wondrous than we'd ever imagined; the geographic distance we traveled fades to insignificance alongside the spiritual heights we scaled.

The bamboo cradle that gently rocked our tiny Chinese daughter to sleep came to symbolize our own beginnings in the discovery of our heritage. In the land where bamboo fields whisper echoes of the sea, we heard a voice calling us home. We did not know then that the voice came from deep within our souls. For the first time, we turned our hearts to God and He answered our prayers. The cradle swayed in the soft China breeze with a will of its own, just as events in our lives created their own momentum.

From our bamboo cradle we emerged into a world of timeless, ancient wisdom. We cut our teeth on Torah and learned to walk with the Prophets; the first words we uttered were words of devotion. Each day dawned on new revelations and faith in the Almighty filled our lives with joy.

We know now that *Hashem*'s hand reaches everywhere. Every event that unfolds, every breath we take, is an expression of His will, yet many deny His very existence. Occasionally the evidence of His active involvement in men's lives is so clear that even the most confirmed skeptic cannot refute His ever-presence and omnipotence. Our story is rich in such evidence. In telling it I hope to inspire the skeptics and others to heed the voice that calls them home, to emerge from their cradle of darkness into a world of light.

PART ONE:

dawn

Weeping may endure for a night,
but with the dawn — joy.

PSALMS 30:6

PROLOGUE

WITH EACH passing minute of the early morning, more and more people poured in and out of the train station. The traffic noise swelled as motor scooters and bicycles merged with buses, cars and taxis. Su-Yen huddled in a doorway opposite the station. She stood alone and still, apart from the moving stream of hurrying figures. She raised her eyes to the large clock above the entrance to the terminal. Six-thirty-five. Soon, she thought, the station would be at its busiest.

A pre-dawn drizzle had mingled with the ever-present dust, and the city was shrouded in a low mist. Su-Yen had been waiting in the doorway since daybreak and had watched the moon give way to the sun as it rose above the East Gate. Although the morning chill had left the air, Su-Yen shivered and drew her thin silk jacket tightly around her. Her heart was quiet, like the dark water of the pond near her grandfather's country home. Feelings and thoughts intertwined. Her mind wandered. She hardly saw the people who passed her on the pavement — two elderly women dressed in black shuffled by, their tiny feet deformed from years of binding; uniformed school children, chattering like jaybirds, hopped and skipped along the sidewalk; a vendor, bent low by the weight of his wares, proffered a bright bird in a woven cage.

A cry, light as a whisper, rose from the small bundle Su-Yen held to her chest and she flinched as if awakened suddenly from a deep dream. How tired and alone she felt. A wave of pain and exhaustion washed over her. The cry became stronger. Su-Yen looked down. The baby's face was damp and bright from her tears.

PROFESSOR ALLAN SCHWARTZBAUM always left his house at 5:45 A.M. on Thursdays. One day each week he traveled to Taichung in central Taiwan. It was a long trip, made even longer by the fact that he had to travel first from the small fishing village of Tamsui to Taipei, and from there take a two-and-a-half-hour train ride to the university. A visiting American professor on a Fulbright Scholarship to the Republic of China, Schwartzbaum held part-time positions in three universities throughout the country, teaching sociology and industrial relations. The quaint hilltop quarters he and his wife, Barbara, occupied in Tamsui had been graciously provided by his Chinese hosts.

As he left the house that morning, he paused to appreciate the special beauty of the early hour. The departing May rains which came in from the China Sea had left a white curtain of clouds on the mountains. The final moments of night were black against a green-red sky. As he walked down the narrow mountain path, he became aware of the activity below. Food stalls were setting up to serve white bean soup and crisp bread. Farmers with their oxen were already specks of moving color in their fields of rice. Sleepy cats and dogs, rising to greet the dawn, stretched with great yawns, and in the distance, behind the willows, the words of a song turned in the air.

Su-Yen knew she must act now. If things had only been different, if the baby had been a boy, if their backgrounds had not been so unalike... A sharp pain interrupted her thoughts. She knew what she had to do, and procrastinating only postponed the inevitable. There was no choice — events had overpowered her. She remembered the old Chinese phrase, "a rushing wave already broken."

She reached into a small bag and found a pen and scrap of paper on which to write a few words. Then, clutching her baby, she strode purposefully toward the station.

THERE WERE SEVERAL ways one could travel from Tamsui. The fastest, but least relaxing, was with one of the special Tamsui-Taipei shuttle taxis, the drivers of which maximized their income by making as many round trips as they could each day. Because of the reckless manner in which the drivers navigated the winding roads at breakneck speeds, these taxis became known as "wild chickens." Buses were safer by far. A third mode of transportation was the local train, which, although it made many stops along the way, conveniently deposited its passengers right at the main train terminal.

Halfway down the mountain path, Schwartzbaum decided he would take the train this morning. He enjoyed sharing the ride with the many schoolchildren who usually rode to the city at that hour. This morning was no exception. Knots of children in twos, threes and fours, schoolbooks strapped on their backs, hopped, pushed, skipped and otherwise made their way into the train compartment. Whenever he watched them, he always discovered a smile on his face.

But the smile quickly faded when he remembered his own situation. He and Barbara had been married for seven years. They led busy, interesting lives traveling, working and studying. But in their quiet moments, when all around them was still, they would feel the palpable silence and vast emptiness that only a child could fill.

As she entered the station, Su-Yen's senses were assaulted by the noise and movement of the crowds all around her. She searched vainly for an empty space or corner where she could leave her bundle, a place where she would not be seen aban-

doning it, but where it was certain to be found.

She slipped off her jacket and wrapped it around the baby, making sure the note was in the pocket. Just then, an announcement came over the public address system, echoing throughout the terminal. A number of commuters rose from the benches and moved like a ragged army towards the platform and their train. For a moment, to Su-Yen's right, there was an unoccupied bench. Quickly, she placed the red jacket with its contents there, then drifted away, blending easily into the milling crowd. Her arms and heart were empty.

SCHWARTZBAUM JOINED the crowd climbing the stairs from the local platform to the main terminal. He purchased his ticket to Taichung, then headed across the huge hall toward his assigned gate. Suddenly, a bright splash of color caught his eye, a small red parcel on a vacant bench. He thought he saw it move. His curiosity piqued, he decided to investigate.

Tiny dark eyes met his own. His briefcase fell from his hand as he reached for the baby. He picked her up gently and held her close. A note fluttered to the ground.

A short distance away, a figure stood watching the foreigner at the bench. After a moment, Su-Yen moved silently away.

THE OFFICE of the railroad police was small but neat and orderly, as was its sole occupant. Lt. Lee glanced up from the report he was writing. He removed his glasses before he spoke. His tone and expression were courteous, but I sensed they concealed a deep-seated cautiousness.

"We apologize for this most unfortunate event," he began. "It is not proper for a distinguished visitor to be involved in such things. We have taken the baby to where she will be looked after. This has inconvenienced you. Let us not trouble you any longer." It seemed I was being dismissed, but my curiosity was far from satisfied.

"Is the baby all right?" I asked.

"She seemed healthy. A doctor will examine her."

"She was so tiny, she could hardly have been more than a few days old."

"It is obvious that she was just born," the lieutenant agreed. "Her umbilical cord was still attached. But she appears strong."

"Does this happen often? I mean, are infants often abandoned like this?"

"Not as often as in the past. Traditionally, sons have been valued far more than daughters. A husband could divorce his wife if she failed to give him sons." I nodded, recalling having read this somewhere. Lee went on. "I remember on the Mainland, when there was nothing to eat, things were so bad that parents would try to sell their children, especially their girls. But here life is much better."

"Then why would someone do such a thing?"

"Perhaps because of 'face', what you would call shame. The mother would not wish to bring shame to her family. If the baby were a boy who could carry the family name, an arrangement might have been worked out, but with a girl...." The lieutenant rose from his stiff-backed chair.

"Before I go," I said, "please let me know where the baby was taken." Lt. Lee hesitated, and looked away. Then he wrote out an address in his precise script and passed it across the desk. "One more question, please. There was a note with the baby. What did it say?"

Again Lee hesitated. "It said: 'Whoever finds this baby — watch over her with kindness and compassion, and fortune will share your way'."

THAT EVENING, Barbara and I sat in the living room of our little house in the faculty housing compound. We loved the house, even though it was sparsely furnished and very simple in design. Like the other faculty structures, it had plain exterior walls, a grey shingle roof and a blood-red door. Tatami mats covered the bare wood floors of the two bed-rooms, but the living room had a couch of sorts and after our evening meal we liked to have tea there. From the window, above a dense stand of bamboo, one could see the fishing boats returning home, tiny beacons of light pinpointed on the bay.

"I felt so strange when I realized it was a baby," I said, breaking the long silence that followed my account of the day's events. "I was frightened, but somehow happy."

Barbara turned toward me. Her eyes glistened. "Do you know where she is now?"

View from our faculty compound residence.

"Yes, the police officer gave me the address of the orphanage — it's on Chung Hwa Road."

"We'll go there first thing tomorrow morning," she said, reading my thoughts. I nodded my agreement. "Yes, first thing."

As we rose from the couch, we noticed that there were no more lights on the water. All the boats had come safely into port.

WHEN WE ARRIVED at the address on Chung Hwa Road at half past eight the next morning, we were surprised to discover that it was a church. We wandered around the stone courtyard for several minutes, until we found an open back door leading to a winding flight of wooden stairs. On the second floor landing, Barbara hesitantly opened a heavy ornate door. Suddenly, the din of countless crying babies assailed us and we were nearly overcome by the fetor of unchanged diapers. The large, high-ceilinged room in which we found ourselves was filled with rows of old-fashioned metal cribs, most of them occupied by wailing infants. There were no caretakers in evidence.

Eventually, a tired-looking woman entered through a narrow doorway. I immediately approached her.

"Good morning," I said over the racket. "We would like to see the baby who was found at the railroad station yesterday."

"Oh! I think she is over in the fourth row, near the wall, somewhere in the middle." She pointed vaguely in that direction and then went about her business.

Barbara and I anxiously searched among the cribs until we found one with a newborn in it. We saw a head of jet black hair and tiny, delicate features. The woman joined us at the crib. "Yes, this is the one. She was brought in just the other day."

"Are you the only person taking care of all these children?" Barbara asked, somewhat appalled.

"Yes. Sometimes I find someone to help me, but usually I am alone."

"How on earth do you manage?"

"Well, I get to each child when I can. They all get taken care of sooner or later."

Barbara turned to me and whispered urgently, "We must get this baby out of here!"

"I found this baby yesterday," I said to the caretaker, again shouting over the noise. "We wish to take her home with us."

"You must speak to Reverend Wen. He is downstairs, in his office."

We located the office and knocked on the door. The gentleman seated at the large desk was tall and balding, his shoulders slightly stooped and his expression blank. He moved slowly, like an old tortoise disturbed from its slumber. "Can I help you?"

"Yes, I hope so. I am Professor Allan Schwartzbaum and this is my wife, Barbara. Yesterday, I found a newborn baby at the railroad station. We were told she was brought here and we've just seen her upstairs. We'd like to take her home with us."

Reverend Wen looked us over very carefully for what seemed like a long time. "It might be possible," he said in a tone that matched his plodding movements, "but it is customary for people to first make a contribution to our church before we provide them with a child. I am sure you understand how expensive it is to care for so many children."

"I see. Please allow me a moment to discuss this with my wife." I took Barbara aside and spoke quietly to her. "I'm fairly certain this guy gives babies to the highest bidder," I said. "He gets unwanted babies, then tries to sell them to anyone who'll pay. What should we do?"

"Make him an offer."

"How much should I say?"

"I don't know, but we must get the baby out of this place immediately."

I turned back to the desk. "Reverend Wen, I have twenty-five U.S. dollars and I'll pay you an additional two hundred dollars by next week." The Reverend looked up but his expression remained impassive. I couldn't tell if I'd bid too high or too low.

"Very good," he said at last. "Please sign this document which indicates how much you promise to give for a contribution." I complied and he took the signed paper, folded it neatly and placed it in one of the desk drawers. "I now release the baby into your care. Since the infant was abandoned we do not know what her family name is. In such cases I list the baby under my surname — Wen. I will also give her a personal name." He looked up at the ceiling, thinking, then wrote several Chinese characters on a sheet of paper before him and announced, "I have named her Yu-Bing — Jade Ice. Her full name is Wen Yu-Bing." He handed the sheet of paper to me and we all went back up the stairs.

Reverend Wen addressed the caretaker. "Professor Schwartzbaum and his wife are going to take this baby with them." The caretaker reached over the rail of the crib and wrapped the baby in a thin blanket. She picked her up and handed her to Barbara without a word. Clearly, this was their routine procedure. I nodded to Reverend Wen and led Barbara down the stairs and out the door, the tiny bundle clutched in her arms.

As we walked out to the church courtyard, I shook my head in amazement. "I don't believe what just happened!" I said. "Can you imagine going into an orphanage in America and walking out a few minutes later with a baby?"

Barbara looked down at the baby who was sleeping peacefully in her arms. "What are we going to do now?"

"Let's get her home — before someone changes his mind!" I flagged down a passing taxi and we climbed in. The driver looked at us curiously but only asked, *"Dau nali chyu?* — Where to?"

"Tamsui."

As the taxi sped past the city limits, Barbara murmured in a soft voice, almost to herself, *"Yu-Bing,* Jade Ice — what a terrible name! It's so cold, so remote." She looked down at the sleeping baby cradled in her arms. "I will never use that name again."

MEI-MEI, OUR HOUSEKEEPER, was busy in the kitchen — as usual — when we returned. Without even a glance in our direction, she declared, "I must be working too hard. I am sure I hear baby crying. Dr. Schwartzbaum, you are joking me again with your funny tricks?"

"Look, Mei-Mei!" Barbara called excitedly. "It *is* a baby! You remember — the baby that Allan found in the train station yesterday? We went to see if we could take her, and here she is!"

Mei-Mei calmly lifted a corner of the little blanket. "You are right," she stated simply, "it is baby — *Chinese* baby. There is old Chinese saying, 'Do not call a tree a rock.' Now tell me, please, what you are going to do with her?"

All at once, the full impact of our actions struck us. Most husbands and wives have nine months to prepare for a new baby. Even when couples adopt, there are many months of interviews, discussions and planning before they ever receive a child. In our case, we awoke that very morning, a childless couple, and three hours later, with no advance preparation, we had an infant.

"What are we going to do?" Barbara cried, a note of panic in her voice. "We have no crib, we have no baby clothes, we don't even have any baby food!"

"You forgot to mention experience," I added. "We don't have any of that, either."

"Do not worry," said Mei-Mei, her round, peasant face glowing with pleasure. "I have plenty experience, and soon you will know what to do also. There is old Chinese saying, 'The hungry child does not need to be taught how to eat'!"

Mei-Mei soon had everything organized. She rounded up the neighbors, and then, almost as if by magic, all the necessities began to appear: a tiny dress, a stock of diapers, an old bamboo cradle, warm blankets, baby bottles. Mei-Mei sent her oldest daughter, who'd been helping in the kitchen, to the market to search for infant formula. When she returned, we were all set.

In no time at all, the news had spread throughout the local community. Heads of curious little children popped up out of nowhere, with everyone trying to get a glimpse of the new baby. A steady stream of neighbors poured through our house, and with it, a steady stream of advice on every subject. After a while, the commotion became so great that Barbara had Mei-Mei bar any more visitors.

The baby seemed healthy. She drank from her bottle and responded to everyone who held her. She also cried. Not little whimpering sounds, but big, robust cries that filled the whole house and reverberated off the walls. Barbara grew anxious. The more she tried to calm the baby, the louder the baby cried. "Mei-Mei! Mei-Mei! What's wrong? Why is she crying? Is she hungry? Maybe she's not well! Maybe something hurts her!"

Mei-Mei answered without interrupting her chores. "Do not worry. It is normal. There is old Chinese saying, 'A silent brook has no water'."

MUCH LATER, when the sun had settled behind the green mountains, and the baby had finally stopped crying, Barbara regained her composure. "We have to have a name for this baby," she said. "We can't keep on calling her 'the baby', and

I absolutely refuse to call her 'Jade Ice'."

"Yes," I said, "I've been giving the subject a lot of thought. Here we are with a tiny Chinese infant, and we have no idea what her future will be, or how her life will turn out. But whatever is in store for her, it began here in China. I'd like to call her 'Hsin-Mei', *Hsin* for heart and *Mei* for China. Hsin-Mei — 'My heart is in China'."

Barbara repeated the name, "Hsin-Mei. Hsin-Mei. Yes, I like it. It suits her."

The baby, as though responding to her new name, began to cry again. "Oh, no!" Barbara exclaimed. "I don't know if I can take any more! All she does is cry!"

"Well, I don't know about you," I said, "but I'm going to sleep."

"But, Allan! Mei-Mei has gone home to her own family. She won't be back until morning! Are you going to leave me all alone with the baby?"

"You bet — the joys of motherhood are all yours. Have a good night!"

Barbara glared at me. "Okay, then — go to sleep. There is old Chinese saying, 'At night, the donkey does not need a lantern to find its stall'!"

O N THE EIGHTH of May, two days after finding the baby, I visited the U.S. Embassy to learn what procedures were required for bringing her home with us when we returned to the States. We had originally planned on leaving Taiwan at the end of June, so time was short and I was anxious to complete the necessary paperwork. An embassy official explained that there were in fact a number of steps to follow before a visa could be issued, but the process could not be initiated until we presented documents showing that the baby had been legally adopted according to Chinese law.

From the Embassy, I went to consult an acquaintance who was a lawyer about the procedures required for a legal Chinese adoption. He told me I had to bring to the Taipei Central Court a birth certificate, along with proof that the child's relatives did not object to the adoption, and a certificate of release from the orphanage. If all the papers were in order, the Court would then issue an official document of adoption.

That afternoon, I returned to the church on Chung Hwa Road and found Reverend Wen seated in his office. He looked up from his paperwork and inquired, "You have been able perhaps to bring the remainder of your contribution?"

"I will definitely attend to the matter in the next day or two," I replied. "Today, I'm trying to complete the requirements for adoption. I need the baby's birth certificate as well as a certificate of release from the orphanage."

I had been expecting him to give me a hard time, but Wen simply removed his ink pad from a drawer in his desk and reached for one of his Chinese pens. He wrote a brief letter, stamped it with his personal seal, and handed it to me. "This will serve as a certificate of release from the orphanage," he said in that slow, impassive tone of his that I found so grating. "Since the baby was found in the railway station, you must obtain a letter from the railway police. This letter will then have to be taken to the appropriate government office which will prepare the birth certificate."

Then he raised his expressionless eyes to mine. The atmosphere in the room became decidedly chilly. "Would it be possible to bring the remainder of the contribution to the church tomorrow morning?" It was more an order than a request.

"As soon as I receive the adoption papers from the court," I assured him, "I will be happy to provide the balance of my contribution." My response did not seem to please him but he only nodded his head slightly and returned to the work on his desk.

Stuffing the letter into my pocket, I rushed out of Wen's oppressive office to the fresh spring air of the courtyard.

PROMPTLY AT EIGHT the following morning, I returned to the railway police station and found myself once again across the desk from the neat, compact Lt. Lee. He had dropped his cautious air and was interested to learn all that had happened since our last meeting. Our choice of the name Hsin-Mei for the baby brought a smile to his face. He volunteered to assist me in obtaining a birth certificate.

"How would one go about determining if the baby had relatives who might want to care for her?" I asked.

Lee reached for a newspaper on a table behind his desk and pointed to a column on page two. "Yesterday's paper reported that a baby was found in the central train station," he said, indicating the news item. "This column instructs anyone having information about the child or any of its relatives to contact this office immediately. This is standard procedure in such cases."

His words sent a shiver down my spine as I realized that Hsin-Mei might not have been abandoned by her parents, but by a nursemaid. The note that had accompanied her was unsigned. Another possibility was that if her mother had in fact abandoned her, upon reading the newspaper notice she might regret her actions and try to retrieve her baby. I suppose I should have been prepared for this eventuality — an adoption could not possibly proceed so swiftly and smoothly as Hsin-Mei's had.

But in the three days since I'd found her, Hsin-Mei had become a very precious part of us. I was suddenly very frightened. I cleared my throat and, trying to sound casual, asked the lieutenant, "Has anyone contacted you?"

Lt. Lee removed his glasses and answered softly, "There has been only silence." We sat quietly for a moment, savoring his response and feeling a bit like co-conspirators. Then Lee placed some papers in an envelope and rose from his chair. "Let us now try to obtain the birth certificate."

We left his tidy office behind us and entered the noisy confusion of the railroad terminal. "My car is parked around the corner and down the street," he said as we threaded our way among the milling passengers, vendors and porters.

When we emerged from the dimly-lit terminal, the bright morning sun greeted us warmly. It was no less crowded out on the street. There was barely room on the sidewalk for the throngs of pedestrians and the bundles and packages of every size and description which they toted. The people moved like a living river and we were carried along the streets of Taipei in the current. Eventually, we found our way to the car.

LEE WAS AS courteous behind the wheel as he was behind his

desk. He skillfully navigated his vehicle through the maze of sidestreets and narrow alleyways that led to the government Population Registry Office, a plain, brown two-story building indistinguishable from those on either side of it.

Addressing the receptionist, Lee explained why we had come and we were escorted to a small lounge area. A young girl appeared and set down two glasses of tea before us. After about ten minutes, we were led into a large high-ceilinged room and directed to a small desk on the left. The clerk in attendance politely offered us glasses of Chinese tea. Lee again explained the purpose of our call and the clerk inspected the documents Lee had presented. Then he rose and asked us to accompany him to a somewhat larger desk on the right side of the room.

No sooner had we taken our seats than two new glasses of tea were brought and the entire process repeated itself. The second clerk excused himself and knocked on the door of a private office at the back of the room. He disappeared into the office and reappeared five minutes later. Then he asked us to follow him to the office of the director of the bureau.

This time, the tea was served in ornate porcelain cups instead of glasses. Clearly, we were making progress.

I couldn't follow Lee's rapid conversation with the director, who glanced up at me from time to time during a pause in their discussion. So I sat there fidgeting, playing with my cup and, every now and then, taking a sip of the pungent green tea. At last the director reached for his phone and issued a series of instructions. Taking my signal from Lee, I rose with him and bowed slightly to the director, thanking him for his assistance and kindness.

On our way out, we stopped at a high counter where a female clerk handed us the original and two copies of a document. Lee examined them carefully, then explained, "This states that Wen Yu-Bing was born on May 6, 1972 in Taipei, Taiwan, Republic of China. Regrettably, since the document from the orphanage had the baby's name listed as

Yu-Bing, it was impossible to change it on the birth certificate."

"I don't think it really matters at this point," I said. "We can legally change the name at a later time. I'll tell my wife that if she wants to pursue the name change, she'll have to be prepared to drink about twenty glasses of tea!"

S EVERAL DAYS LATER, while Mei-Mei watched the baby, Barbara and I went to Taipei, to the Central Court. I took along a leather folder containing the birth certificate, a copy of the newspaper announcement seeking information about the child found in the railway station, and the signed release from the orphanage. I was pleased with the progress I had made so far, cutting through the bureaucratic red tape. "After our session today," I told Barbara, "all that'll be left is getting a visa from the U.S. Embassy, and we'll be able to leave on schedule at the end of June."

Unlike the government registry office, the Central Court was housed in an impressive stone building. The receptionist directed us down a long corridor to a very small chamber off the main hall, where a clerk collected our papers and asked us to be seated. Soon a distinguished looking individual, who we assumed was the judge, entered the now crowded chamber. We knew all the papers were in order so we simply sat there, calmly awaiting the judge's approval.

The judge bent over the documents and inspected each item closely. Suddenly he looked up and rose stiffly from his chair. He spoke sharply. "I will not approve this adoption. It is unacceptable." Tall and erect, he strode from the room. The clerk followed him. The room which only seconds ago had seemed so crowded and full of promise was now empty and silent. We were stunned.

After a few minutes, the clerk returned. "What went wrong? What's the problem?" Barbara asked anxiously.

"The judge will not deal with Reverend Wen," the clerk explained. "Wen is a man of low character and poor reputation. The judge knows this person from previous cases. He will have nothing to do with him. He became angry when he saw the signature on the certificate and so he left the chamber."

"Well, what can we do now?"

"You must bring the baby to another orphanage, one which is on an approved government list, as is not the case with Reverend Wen's. You must bring a certificate of release from an approved institution."

"But we already have the baby at home with us!" Barbara exclaimed.

"This is a matter to take up with the orphanage," the clerk replied. "They may require you to give the baby over into their care until you make an application for adoption and the matter is resolved." He bowed slightly, indicating the end of the discussion.

We left the chamber and trudged slowly down the long stone corridor, engulfed in a sea of despair.

ONCE AGAIN I found myself walking through the train terminal to the railway police station, this time with a very dejected looking wife at my side. I had to struggle to keep the note of strain from my voice as I questioned Lt. Lee. "How could this happen?" I demanded to know. "How did the baby wind up in Reverend Wen's orphanage if it's unregistered? The judge in the Central Court will have nothing to do with our case because of that man's reputation."

Lee shifted in his seat uncomfortably, but I ignored it and went on. "The baby was found here at the railway station — which is under *your* jurisdiction. After I found the baby I turned her over to one of *your* men. How did she land at Chung Hwa Road, in an unlicensed orphanage, the director of which is in the business of selling babies?"

Lee produced a small card from his desk drawer. The message on the card read, *If children require care, I will look after them in my church. I will reward you for your concern.* "These cards have been widely distributed in places where children are likely to be left — bus and railway stations, markets and parks. This is the primary way that Reverend Wen acquires children for his orphanage. If people bring a child to him, he pays them a small fee. He then exacts a high price from those seeking to adopt. The officer who brought your foundling to his orphanage has already been disciplined. Did you offer Reverend Wen any money for the baby?"

"I'm afraid so, Lieutenant. At his suggestion that I make a 'contribution' to his church, I offered to pay him two hundred and twenty-five dollars. I only gave him twenty-five so far, but he's been asking for the rest."

"Do not pay him a penny more," Lee admonished sternly. "The social services division of the government has launched an investigation because of your case. Once foreigners become involved, everything gets much more complicated."

"Where does that leave my wife and me? What do we do now?"

"I will offer you what assistance I can," Lee replied with an encouraging smile. "If you and your wife will meet me at three o'clock tomorrow with the baby, I will drive you to the main government orphanage. We will see if they will be willing to issue the necessary certificate."

"And if they're not?" I asked.

Lt. Lee quietly replaced Reverend Wen's card in his desk and looked away.

THE DIRECTOR of the government orphanage was a heavyset, middle-aged woman, dressed in the severe black dress traditionally worn by Chinese women of her generation.

Although she had apparently been told to expect our visit, her greeting was as stiff and severe as her attire. Lee introduced us, using our Chinese names — Hsu Bai-Lan and Hsu Hwa-Peng* — and briefly stated the purpose of our visit.

"How long have you considered adoption?" the director asked peremptorily.

Barbara told her we had thought about it off and on, and in fact, before coming to Taiwan, we had inquired about adoption in the U.S. We learned at that time that the waiting list for children was two to four years — and even then there was no assurance that a child would be available. "I always hoped that one day we might have children of our own," Barbara added.

"I see," said the director. "Did you ever consider adopting a Chinese child?"

"We did discuss it once or twice," I replied, "but..."

"But you never came to an approved orphanage," the director interrupted. "Instead you sought out someone who is a disgrace to our profession."

"Well, you do understand the circumstances, don't you?" I said testily. The woman's attitude was extraordinarily offensive. "The child I found was brought by others to Reverend Wen. It was not *our* choice to go there. We were hoping that we could say the baby came from your orphanage and in that way secure the required certificate of release. If necessary, we can actually leave the baby here for a day or two."

The director's smile was unctuous. "Certainly you can leave the infant with us," she said, "where she will be carefully watched over. But we also have a long waiting list of parents who wish to adopt. Once the child is given into our care she must be placed with those parents who are at the top

* Hsu is the family name, an approximation of the first syllable of Schwartzbaum and a common Chinese surname. Bai-Lan means "white orchid". Hwa-Peng means "friend of China". Hsu Hwa-Peng means "promise to be a friend of China."

of the list. You are welcome to add your name to this list and when there is a child available, we will be happy to contact you."

Barbara flew from the office and out onto the street, clutching Hsin-Mei tightly. When Lee and I caught up to her, there were tears streaming down her cheeks. "What a terrible woman," she cried. "I'll never give up this baby, *never!*" I tried to comfort her. The lieutenant stood apart, staring at the ground.

AS SOON AS WE ENTERED the house, Mei-Mei knew something was wrong. Barbara told her the whole story, her voice breaking periodically. Mei-Mei seemed surprisingly unmoved by the account. "It seems to me that baby Hsin-Mei still is here in your arms and not with lady crow," she said with a shrug. "I do not understand. Why you go to different orphanage when you already have baby? There is old Chinese saying, 'Riding a mule to seek a mule'!"

"Don't you see, Mei-Mei?" I shouted in exasperation. "We need a certificate of release from an *approved* orphanage."

"I understand," said Mei-Mei, "but Chinese way is to have someone act for you. To go yourself is like trying to scratch toe with shoe still on foot. People come to visit you all the time — I know, I do cooking! Your doorway is like marketplace. Your students have fathers; these fathers have friends; these friends have friends. The Chinese say, 'When the water rises, the boat rises also'!"

"Well," I said, saluting our wise, wonderful housekeeper, "if our family is a boat, I know who the captain is."

The next morning, Mei-Mei looked on approvingly as I, dressed in my best suit, prepared to leave the house for the day's activities. "Yes, you look like distinguished scholar," she teased. "You are not old enough really and you do not have beard and your hair is not white, but people make exceptions for foreigners." Then her tone became serious.

"Now remember, you are professor who is teaching son or daughter of someone. You want apple in exchange for pears." I nodded to my tutor, called goodbye to Barbara and was out the door.

As I walked hurriedly down the mountain path, I heard Mei-Mei calling to me from the window, "Remember, APPLES!"

MY FIRST STOP WAS at the home of a representative of the Chinese foreign ministry. We chatted amiably for a while about the Fulbright Fellowship program. We discussed some of the many American scholars who had come to Taiwan, and their Chinese counterparts who had been invited to the United States. Near the end of the meeting, I mentioned my new, personal connection to China, and the "small problem" I was having.

Next I visited the father of one of my students at Taiwan National University, a man who just happened to be head supervisor of all social workers in the Taipei area. We, too, had an amiable discussion and exchanged pleasantries.

Later I dropped in at the residence of a distinguished Chinese jurist, a retired judge who was a board member of the U.S.-Republic of China Educational Foundation.

That evening I dined with the parents of a student from Chung Hsing University. The father was an aide to the mayor of Taipei.

When I returned home late that night, I found Barbara anxiously waiting up for me. "You look exhausted," she said. "How did it go? Do you think you accomplished something?"

"I can't be absolutely certain," I answered, "but I feel like..."

"A diplomat?"

"No-o-o..."

"A politician?"

"No-o-o...I feel like...Johnny Appleseed!"

院 幼 育 音 福
GOSPEL CHILDREN'S HOME
(號一四三一箱郵)號三路南山中市北台同中由自：址院
Address: No. 3, S. Chong Shen Rd., Taipei, Free China
(Box 1341) Taipei, Free China Tel. 361856

June 10th '72

[Handwritten letter from Reverend Wen]

Dear Dr. & Mrs. Schwartzkraum:

Due to the staff of City Gov. know that you offer $300 to us for your baby they told all 55 papers reporters that Gospel Orphanage committed selling baby crime & I will face the judges soon & will put to jail for 5 yrs punishment.

Would you please help me by writing a nice letter to explain that $300 1st time (I don't count that now) & $25 each yr was written by yourself willingly & Jordan Wen never request for that or ever set a price for that baby just to help the orphaned kids.

Mr. 陳宗仁 superintendent of Taichung christian orphanage will help you to get all papers for your baby instead of me. His address: 234, 民族路, 台中, write him immediately. Thanks Sincerely

Jordan Wen

P.S. June 8th Eight papers big column of criticizing us, damage our work very much.

IT IS MORE BLESSED TO GIVE THAN TO RECEIVE

Letter from Reverend Wen requesting our intervention on his behalf in his upcoming trial for "selling babies."

LIFE AT THE SCHWARTZBAUM household drifted into a routine: Hsin-Mei began to sleep through the night; Barbara and I continued our studies and research. But despite our efforts, we couldn't conceal our nervousness and concern from one another. We felt ourselves sinking slowly into despair, to the point where even the ever-optimistic Mei-Mei had trouble finding encouraging Chinese sayings to lift our spirits. When Barbara would suddenly burst into tears or launch into a diatribe about the government orphanage that refused to help us, Mei-Mei would draw on her inexhaustible supply of profound proverbs. "Do not worry about lady crow. Chinese say, 'One hand cannot hide the sun.' Anyway, crow cannot do harm now — 'A needle is not sharp at both ends'!"

This tactic of Mei-Mei's, which had successfully gotten us through many rough moments during the past months, was failing dismally now. I became increasingly pessimistic with each passing day, and every time Mei-Mei tried to cheer us up, I would match her heartening maxims with a disheartening one of my own. When she repeated the adage about the rising water lifting the boat, I countered with: "Water floats a boat; it also sinks it."

Late one sleepless night, I stepped outside on our veranda. The night air was still. Above me loomed the moon-streaked mountain, while the sea rose and fell below. A hanging lantern swung slowly in a brief summer breeze, making shadows dance by its side. Beyond the light, darkness filled the fields and rice paddies. I watched the bamboo tremble once and reach for an overhanging pine, while the sound of a distant temple bell mingled with a baby's whimper, leaving brushstrokes in the dark. From deep within me, I prayed.

WEEKS PASSED. Then early one morning, we received a message to contact Lt. Lee. I called immediately. "Please join me as soon as possible at the railway police station," he said without preamble. "Bring Hsin-Mei and your wife."

"What's happening?" I asked.

"I will explain later. Goodbye."

In twenty minutes' time we were aboard a "wild chicken" taxi to Taipei. As soon as we walked into Lee's office, he jumped out of his chair and led us to his car. "We are going to another orphanage," he called over his shoulder.

We crossed the bridge which separated Taipei from its suburbs and eventually arrived at a dull grey building. When we passed through the heavy wood doors, we found ourselves surrounded at once by flocks of smiling, curious children.

A woman came out to meet us. She introduced herself as Mrs. Chou and invited us into her office. Naturally, tea was served and we sipped it politely while Mrs. Chou wrote out a letter and stamped it with her seal. "This is a certificate of release for your daughter," she explained, handing me the document.

"Do we have to leave Hsin-Mei with you?" Barbara asked hesitantly.

"That will not be necessary," Mrs. Chou replied.

"Thank you ever, ever so much," Barbara gushed, unable to contain her excitement and happiness. "This is wonderful, you are so kind." We all rose and Lee and I bowed slightly, thanking Mrs. Chou for her trouble. The three of us walked out of the orphanage grinning from ear to ear.

Lee drove us to a bus station from where we would have no trouble getting home. We thanked him for all his help, but the words seemed hopelessly inadequate. "There is one more thing," he said, slipping an envelope out of his inside pocket.

"What is this?" I asked.

"You may open it."

In the envelope was twenty-five dollars.

Chapter 6

I T HAD TAKEN twenty-eight anguish-filled days to secure Hsin-Mei's official adoption papers from the
Chinese court, but that was all behind us now. The
visa was our next hurdle, so I made an appointment
with the consular officer at the U.S. Embassy.

After breakfast, Barbara's Chinese language teacher, Chiang Lau-Shr* called at the house. Chiang Lau-Shr was actually far more than a language teacher. She had become a very
close friend who helped us interpret the intricate and often
perplexing Chinese world of which we were now a part.

The Chinese language consists of over one hundred dialects. These dialects differ so greatly that they are almost
separate languages. A person living in one area of China is
often unable to carry on a conversation with someone from
another area. Although each dialect of Chinese has its own
pronunciation, Chinese is written the same way throughout
China. Many Chinese can only communicate with one
another by writing. The most common dialect of Chinese is
Mandarin, often referred to as *p'u-t'ung hwa* or Standard
Chinese, and the highest standard of Mandarin is spoken in
Peking.

* Lau-Shr means "teacher" in Chinese and is a term of respect and defer-
ence similar to calling someone *morah* in Hebrew.

Chiang Lau-Shr was born in Mongolia and her family moved to Peking when she was a small child. One could easily see evidence of her Mandarin lineage in her strong, sharp facial features and athletic build, but she still wore her hair clipped like a school girl's, just as she must have worn it years ago. Listening to Chiang Lau-Shr speak Chinese was like listening to music. She was a radio announcer in addition to being a teacher, and was well-known for her light, melodic voice.

In Barbara, Chiang Lau-Shr had discovered a naturally gifted student and with relentless urging and coaxing, she'd succeeded in getting Barbara to participate in a national contest for foreign students of Chinese. Each contestant had had to present a five-minute speech in Chinese to a panel of judges. Barbara had been awarded second prize, and ever since, she and Chiang Lau-Shr had been the closest of friends.

Chiang Lau-Shr had come to Taiwan in 1949 with over one-and-a-half million refugees who were fleeing the mainland after the Communist takeover. When these Mainlanders arrived, there were already about twelve million Chinese or Taiwanese living on the island. Their ancestors had migrated to Taiwan in the seventeenth century from Fukien and Kwangtung provinces on the mainland. The Taiwanese speak a different dialect from the Mainlanders and have developed their own native culture. They also differ somewhat in appearance. For many years, relations between the two groups have been strained and distant.

This tension occasionally evinced itself in matters concerning Hsin-Mei's care. The Taiwanese make sure that all infants sleep on their backs since they fear a baby might suffocate if positioned on its stomach. As a result of constantly lying this way while their bones are still soft, Taiwanese infants become distinctly flat-headed. Mainlanders don't subscribe to this practice, and in fact deliberately allow their babies to sleep on their stomachs.

Whenever Chiang Lau-Shr visited, the first thing she would do was head for Hsin-Mei's cradle and turn her over onto her stomach. After a few minutes, Mei-Mei, a Taiwanese, would reverse Hsin-Mei's position. Until Barbara realized what was going on, she could not for the life of her understand how tiny Hsin-Mei kept rotating every few minutes.

On this particular morning, Chiang Lau-Shr came to inform Barbara that it was a Chinese custom to celebrate the completion of a baby's first month. This ceremony, called *man ywe* (literally, "full month") required special foods and cakes which she helped Barbara prepare.

On the day of the ceremony, a large group gathered at our home to commemorate the first month of life of an infant whose origins were as unclear as her future. Chiang Lau-Shr stayed on after the other guests departed. She and Mei-Mei began to speculate whether Hsin-Mei was a Taiwanese or a Mainlander. Each took turns offering physiological evidence to support her position. Chiang Lau-Shr pointed to Hsin-Mei's tiny nose as proof that she was a Mainlander. Mei-Mei countered by citing the shape of the face.

"Isn't it possible that one parent was a Mainlander and one a Taiwanese?" Barbara suggested. "This might explain why it was necessary for the biological mother to give her up. If this is the case, Hsin-Mei represents the best of two Chinese worlds."

About an hour later, I wandered into the kitchen. Mei-Mei and Chiang Lau-Shr were deep in conversation, their animated faces warm and friendly as they drank their tea.

WHEN I WENT to the American Embassy, I brought along the adoption papers and Hsin-Mei's chest X-ray, as I had been told to do over the phone. The consular officer to whom I handed the materials commented that everything looked in order. Then he added, "Now, all we need to do is wait for the arrival of the special investigative officer."

This unexpected remark caught me off guard. *"What* investigative officer?" I asked.

"Oh, I thought I had explained this to you earlier," he said casually. "Whenever we have a request for a visa in a case like this, the Department of Immigration and Naturalization requires an investigation of the background of the individuals who wish to bring the child into the United States. Unfortunately, there have been abuses in the past, instances where individuals pretending to act with the very best motives have brought children from foreign countries into the U.S. for the purpose of exploiting them in the most tragic ways. Therefore, we require that you provide references, that is, people who knew you in your home community and that a special officer personally interview you and your wife."

"How long does all this take?"

"Generally six months, sometimes longer."

"Six months!" I exclaimed. "My grant runs out at the end of this month. I'm starting a new job in a new city in the States in a month and a half!"

"Well, it may be possible, because of the extenuating circumstances, to accelerate the process, but it is absolutely essential for you to be interviewed by the investigative officer. This requirement cannot be waived."

"Fine. I accept this. When can we meet with him?"

"I'm afraid there is only one such officer for the Far East. Too bad — he was here three weeks ago. He's in Okinawa now."

I inhaled and exhaled deeply, controlling my rising temper. "And when will he be returning to Taiwan?"

"I believe he's expected back some time near the end of August. Listen, let me cable him and ask him what can be done in your case."

Once again we were awash in a tide of red tape. Barbara tried to contain her disappointment when I reviewed the day's frustrating events for her over supper that evening. Later in the week I discussed the situation with the Fulbright board and they generously agreed to extend my grant for another month. In the meantime, the Embassy called to say that we should forward all the necessary forms to Japan, the investigative officer's next stop. This would enable him to initiate the required procedures prior to his arrival in Taiwan. We promptly completed all the paperwork, including the provision of names of references in the U.S., and the information was dispatched to Japan in the next diplomatic pouch. Then there was nothing more for us to do but wait for matters to take their course.

I contacted the Embassy in July to learn how things were progressing. The consular officer promised to check. The following day, he called back to say that the materials had somehow been misplaced. Two days later he called again — the file had been relocated. Bureaucracy had us firmly in its grip.

Finally, in the middle of August, the investigative officer arrived in Taiwan. The interview proceeded very smoothly. I returned to the Embassy the next day and received Hsin-Mei's visa, just like that. Six days after, the three of us were at the airport, boarding a China Airlines flight to New York.

YEARS LATER, when examining the diary she had kept during this period in Taiwan, Barbara discovered that on that particular Sunday morning when we departed for the West, in Israel and the U.S. it was still Shabbos, and the *haftarah* that was read that day began, "Sing, O barren one, you who have borne no child! Break into song and cry aloud... for the children of the abandoned outnumber those of the married wife...." (Isaiah 54:1).

PART TWO:

first light

*Then shall Your light break forth
like the dawn; and Your
healing shall spring forth quickly...*

ISAIAH 58:8

AFTER OUR months-long roller coaster ride of bureaucratic ups and downs and our tumultuous paper chase through a gaggle of governmental departments, Barbara and I were totally drained. We sat on the plane in a stupor, physically and emotionally exhausted.

The flight to New York was long and tiring. We had to change planes in Japan and there were stopovers in Guam and Alaska. At last the plane landed at Kennedy International Airport in New York.

Barbara's parents and my mother were waiting to greet us. It was during the delay involved in clearing passport control and customs that we first began to worry about our parents' reaction to their new Chinese granddaughter. From the outset, all the decisions we'd made regarding Hsin-Mei had been totally spontaneous; we'd followed our hearts, not our heads. There had been no logical calculations or thoughts about the ramifications of our actions. Now we were about to present our parents with a tiny *fait accompli* who did not look at all like any other member of the family and whose origins were completely unknown.

The reunion was joyous and tearful. Back in the warm embrace of our family, we felt all the fears and doubts dissolve as the new grandmothers took turns cuddling Hsin-

Mei as though she were their own flesh and blood. The general consensus was that the baby was adorable and that Barbara and I had gotten much too thin.

It was impossible to relate all the events and answer the barrage of questions during the car ride to Barbara's parents' home in Coney Island. After bringing our belongings up to the apartment, we sat and talked until late into the evening, and then Barbara and I surrendered to fatigue. The tolling of the bell buoy offshore and the cooing of the grandmothers over their new charge were the last sounds we heard before sleep overwhelmed us.

"Hsin-Mei" examines her new environment.

WE'D BEEN TERRIBLY neglectful of our correspondence over the past year and our families were hungry for details of our life and experiences in China. Relations and friends came to visit and the next ten days were filled with our telling and

retelling of stories and anecdotes from our thirteen months
abroad. At the same time, we were preparing for our immi-
nent departure to a distant city where I would be assuming a
new position as associate professor of sociology and anthropology. As one might imagine, the apartment was in a state
of perpetual turmoil.

Hsin-Mei, however, accepted her hectic new environment with total equanimity and seemed remarkably calm for
a three-month-old who had just traveled halfway around the
world. She was unperturbed by the parade of people who
wanted to see and hold her.

A number of the visitors were family members we hadn't
seen in years, including Barbara's religious relatives. Both
our mothers had been raised in observant Jewish homes but,
as was common among women of their generation, they had

Rochel's father with his new granddaughter.

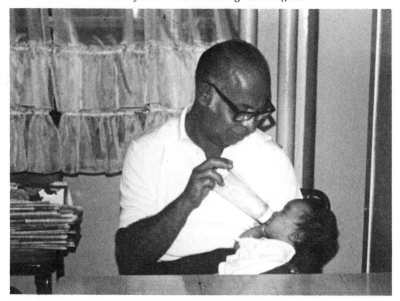

married men from totally secular backgrounds. The results were families which were culturally Jewish, with many of the superficial trappings of Judaism, but which lacked the spirit and depth of religious households. Barbara and I had received a diluted Jewish primary education consisting, in my case, of after-school preparation for Bar Mitzvah and, in Barbara's case, of language and historical studies.

Barbara's mother was one of five daughters and three sons. Six of the eight siblings ranged in observance from traditional to totally secular, while two were Orthodox. As a child, Barbara had been invited to the home of one of these couples for Passover and other holidays, and she retained a close relationship with them, but I noted a coolness and reserve on their part towards Hsin-Mei. This I attributed to their general insularity and narrowness and didn't think of it any further, until years later when I finally understood.

Our visit ended all too quickly. We piled our belongings and Hsin-Mei into our car and began the five-hour drive to our new home. Our parents, sad to see us leave again, were comforted by the fact that this time we were not destined for far-off China. We'd be only a phone call away.

OUR NEW neighborhood was a delightful surprise and quite a change from New York City. It was picturesque and charming with wide tree-lined streets, two-story private homes and spacious yards. Historical landmarks and monuments, churches with spires and steeples, and public parks, gardens and squares surrounded us. The McGraths, close friends of ours, had rented for us a beautiful house bordered by old shade trees and rows of azaleas.

The process of settling in took all of our attention. There were appliances and furniture to be bought, the car had to be registered, arrangements had to be finalized with the telephone and utility companies, and I had to prepare for my new classes at the university. I was sitting in the pine-paneled kitchen one morning, finishing my breakfast coffee, when I happened to glance at the calendar. Rosh Hashanah was exactly one week away.

Although religious observance had never played a major role in our lives, we had always attended the High Holidays services — even in Taiwan, where we joined the American servicemen at the U.S. Army chapel. "What do you think we should do this year about Rosh Hashanah," I asked Barbara, "since we don't belong to any synagogue here?"

"I'm not sure," Barbara answered. "Don't we need to buy

tickets in advance to attend High Holidays services?"

"Wait a minute," I said. "I vaguely remember reading something in yesterday's newspaper about services being conducted at the Jewish Community Center. Let me see if I can find the notice." I rummaged through the papers until I found what I was looking for. "Here it is. 'The Progressive Synagogue—Ohr Emmet* cordially invites the community, including new and unaffiliated members, to worship together with its congregation at the Jewish Community Center. Rosh Hashanah services will be held Thursday morning at ten-thirty. No tickets required.' What do you say?"

"Why not?" Barbara agreed. "We don't seem to have any alternative."

WHEN THE FIRST DAY of Rosh Hashanah arrived, we left Hsin-Mei with a babysitter and headed for the Community Center, about five miles from our home. The Center parking lot was already filling up with cars when we pulled in. "Look at this crowd!" I said. "This must be either an extremely popular synagogue, a very religious city, or a community with a great many unaffiliated Jews."

"Offhand, from the looks of this congregation, I'd say the latter."

The auditorium of the Community Center appeared to be set up for a stage show. Remnants of posters from past events papered the walls and scores of molded plastic chairs were arranged in precise, orderly rows. We looked around the hall at the other worshipers. It was generally a well-dressed gathering of young couples with only a sprinkling of older people and teenagers. I'd put on a yarmulka before entering the hall, but now I saw that few of the other men had done so.

---

* To avoid embarrassment, both to the individuals involved and to myself, many of the names of people and places in this book have been changed.

On each seat there was a packet of mimeographed sheets stapled together. We thumbed through the pages of what we took to be our "prayer books" while we waited for the service to begin. The pamphlets contained an eclectic collection of excerpts from poems by Whitman, Frost, Gibran, Bialik, Milton and Donne, among others; psalms translated into English; literary quotations; songs; and various prayers.

At half past ten, a man in his early thirties addressed the audience. Speaking with a microphone, he introduced himself as president of the congregation. He stated that Congregation Ohr Emmet was one year old and was the result of efforts by a group of families who had joined together to build a modern, progressive congregation that could relate Judaism to the modern world. Their approach, he said, was "polydirectional" and encouraged tolerance, diversity and pluralism. They wished to promote observance without coercion. "If some members wish to wear *kippot* and *tallit*," he declared, "that would be appropriate for them. If others wish to wear *kippot* without *tallit* or *tallit* without *kippot*, that would be proper. And if others wish to dispense with these ritual items altogether, that too would be appropriate."

At this point I leaned over and whispered to Barbara, "And if some wish to wear bells on their shoes, that would also be appropriate." She jabbed me with her elbow.

The spokesman continued, "Our philosophy of polydirectionalism also guides our approach to prayer. The materials which you found on your seats were prepared by the members of our ritual committee. Their selections include inspirational messages from many sources and some original prayers which they prepared themselves. Finally, I want to stress that our congregation maintains, as one of its basic tenets, full gender equality." There was no applause. "Now allow me to introduce our rabbi."

A tall, handsome young man approached the lectern. Like the congregational president, the rabbi was not wear-

At our new suburban home.

ing a yarmulka. He proceeded to lead the service, which consisted of reading either in unison, alternately or silently from the prepared material. For some items, the rabbi would call on individual members of the congregation to lead the assembly.

The readings were interspersed with singing, led by a college girl with a guitar and a pleasant voice. The songs were all familiar and included "Blowin' in the Wind," *"Oseh Shalom,"* "We Shall Overcome" and *"Hinei Ma Tov."*

"I wonder if they take requests?" I muttered and was rewarded with another light jab to the ribs.

Approximately forty-five minutes into the service, the rabbi delivered his sermon. He spoke on the relevance of

Judaism to contemporary issues and problems. He discussed how the Torah, as a collection of ethical insights, emerged in response to pressing dilemmas confronting the ancient Israelites. The task of Jews today, he declared, was to reconstruct this ethical framework so as to provide a basis for resolving current difficulties. The rabbi spoke eloquently for thirty minutes, after which there were fifteen more minutes of reading and song.

At exactly twelve o'clock the president returned to the rostrum. He thanked everyone for coming and invited the gathering to return for the Yom Kippur services.

On our way home, I asked Barbara how she found the service. "A bit alien," she said. "There was hardly any Hebrew. And while I liked some of the readings, the service just seemed to be a series of fragments and passages lumped together. It didn't really move me or affect me. What about you?"

"I felt like I was at a college lecture," I said. "I also didn't find the prayers written by the congregants any improvement over the traditional ones. But I must say I appreciate the fact that this congregation opened its doors to the whole community and tried to make everyone feel welcome."

LATER THAT EVENING, after finishing supper and putting Hsin-Mei to sleep, Barbara was in a pensive mood. "At the service this morning," she said, "something occurred to me. I realized that you and I are Jewish because our parents are Jewish and our parents' parents were Jewish...but what about Hsin-Mei? I remember learning that in order to be Jewish one has to be born to a Jewish woman, and even though we don't know anything about Hsin-Mei's biological mother, it's almost certain she's not Jewish."

"So what you're saying is that you and I are Jewish, but our daughter isn't?"

"Exactly! And the situation is complicated by the fact that Hsin-Mei is Chinese. Because of her racial features, people will always question her Jewishness."

I knew Barbara was right. "What do you think we should do?"

"Well, I imagine the simplest solution would be to convert Hsin-Mei to Judaism. I don't know what's involved with the conversion of a baby, but since both you and I are Jewish, I can't imagine that it's too complicated."

"Who should we approach to do the conversion? We're too new to really know much about the community."

"I think we should go to an Orthodox rabbi," Barbara declared. "That way, later in life no one will be able to question whether or not Hsin-Mei is Jewish because she will have been converted by the strictest, most traditional branch of Judaism."

"There has to be at least one Orthodox synagogue in the city," I said, reaching for the Yellow Pages. "Here it is, under 'Churches — Jewish — Orthodox:' Congregation Shaarei Emmet. Hmm, that's a funny coincidence. It seems most of the congregations in this city have similar names. The congregation we were with today called itself *Ohr* Emmet — the light of truth. The one I just looked up is called *Shaarei* Emmet' — the gates of truth. The directory also lists a Conservative congregation called *Bnei* Emmet — the children of truth. Evidently, everyone claims to have discovered the veritable proven path." I grinned at the irony of it. "I wonder where the truth really lies."

SHORTLY AFTER Rosh Hashanah, I contacted the Orthodox rabbi. He was noncommittal over the telephone, but he consented to meet with us after the High Holidays, so I made an appointment to see him.

The three of us found the rabbi of Shaarei Emmet ensconced in his study, a small room in which every inch of wall space was occupied by books. A large volume was open on his desk. Rabbi Berger was a dark-haired fellow with an impressive beard that covered most of his face, making it difficult to estimate his age. He was probably in his late thirties or early forties. He asked us to be seated.

I explained that the purpose of our visit was to discuss the conversion of our daughter and recounted the story of how we had acquired Hsin-Mei. Since both of us were Jewish, I went on, it was only natural that we wanted our daughter to be Jewish too.

Rabbi Berger listened attentively. When I completed my narrative, he questioned us about our own Jewish background. Barbara reviewed our prior Jewish education. She indicated that we were not particularly observant but that we both had strong, positive feelings about being Jewish.

The rabbi leaned back in his chair, his gaze fixed on the ceiling. After a prolonged pause he said, "You both seem to understand that a child born to a non-Jewish mother has the status of a non-Jew according to Jewish law. The fact that you have legally adopted your daughter, and that you are both Jewish does not alter the religious status of your child. She is not Jewish since ties of blood and kinship can neither be destroyed nor created. The adopted child retains the status of its biological parents."

"Excuse me, Rabbi," Barbara interjected, "why did you just say parents, and not mother alone? I thought it was only the Jewishness of the mother which is relevant to the religious standing of the child."

The rabbi explained that while the mother determines the child's Jewishness, there are certain statuses which are inherited through the father. "If the biological father is a *Kohain* or a *Levi* — a Priest or a Levite," he said, "and the adoptive father is not, or if the adoptive father is a *Kohain* or *Levi* and the biological father is not, the adopted child always retains the same status as his natural father."

I asked about our case, where the child was of totally unknown parentage. "How can one say with absolute certainty that her biological mother was not Jewish? After all, at one time, there were in fact authentic Chinese Jews."

"Yes, the Talmud deals with this issue. There is a category called *asufi*, which refers to a foundling discovered on the street, for whom no one can identify either its father or its mother. The Gemara even deals with a related concept called *shetuki*, where the mother's identity is known but the father's is not. However, that category is not relevant here. In any event, in the case of the *asufi*, we rule according to the majority of the population which, in Taiwan, is gentile. If you were to tell me that there are American servicemen who are stationed in Taiwan or who take their recreational leave in Taiwan, and one of them could have been the biological parent, I will tell you that most of the American military are in fact men, not women, and if there are American servicewomen in Taiwan, the likelihood of their being Jewish is very remote."

I conceded the point and Rabbi Berger continued. "If you had found your daughter in a train station in Tel Aviv, then that would be a completely different story. Believe me when I tell you that in many ways it is much, much simpler if the adoptive child's biological mother is demonstrably non-Jewish. This totally eliminates any question of whether or not the child has the status of *mamzer*, which refers to offspring of certain illicit relationships involving a Jewish mother. Now, as you yourselves have concluded, in order for a non-Jewish adopted child to be regarded as Jewish, he or she must go through a formal conversion."

"What does that entail?" Barbara asked.

"First, the conversion must be done with the approval of and in the presence of a rabbinic court or *beis din* which is comprised of three qualified men. Male children must be circumcised by a competent *mohel* and immersed in an approved or kosher ritual bath called a *mikveh*. For female children, all that is required is immersion in the *mikveh*. A Hebrew name is given to the child and appropriate benedictions are recited by the members of the *beis din*."

That seemed straightforward enough. "How do we proceed with such a conversion for our daughter?"

This time the rabbi hesitated for almost a full minute before responding. "The conversion of a non-Jewish child is a complicated issue in Jewish law. To begin with, the basic requirement is that the candidate for conversion obligate himself or herself to perform all the *mitzvos*. A child before the age of maturity is halachically incompetent to make such a commitment. However, there are several opinions which hold that the *beis din* has sufficient authority to *bestow* Jewishness upon a child, based on the premise that this is essentially equivalent to providing the child with a special privilege, or *zechus*, in Hebrew. Jewish law maintains that one can perform a meritorious deed on behalf of other persons without their consent. Now, the privilege the child receives is the fulfillment one derives from living a full

Jewish life according to the precepts of the Torah.

"Once one becomes a Jew," the rabbi continued, "he is absolutely obligated to observe all the *mitzvos*. Therefore, it would be wrong, in my opinion, to convert a child to Judaism with the knowledge that the child would be situated in a home where these *mitzvos* were not followed, where the Sabbath was not observed, where there was disregard for *kashrus* and all the other precepts of the Torah. If, on the other hand, we were to leave the child a non-Jew, all this would be irrelevant. Non-Jews are not obligated by the same requirements as we are. As long as they follow the limited set of commandments that govern their existence, non-Jews are deemed to be fully righteous and deserving.

"You must try to understand that the issue is not one of race — it wouldn't matter an iota if the child were Chinese, Eskimo or African. The only relevant question is the nature of the home that the child will be living in. In your case, your home does not yet meet the standards of an observant Jewish home."

"In other words, you are not willing to perform the conversion." I was frankly flabbergasted. I would have thought Jews would be happy to welcome a new member into the fold.

"That is my position," Rabbi Berger said, "but if you and your wife wish to study and develop your home into one based on Torah principles, then we can take up the question of conversion again."

"What's involved in this transformation?" Barbara asked.

"We mentioned Shabbos and keeping kosher. There are other laws governing modesty in dress and speech, observing the various festivals and the requirements of prayer, including *tefillin*, to cite just a few. Altogether there are six hundred and thirteen *mitzvos* in the Torah. It requires considerable study and effort, but the rewards are immeasurable."

"I see," Barbara said in a low voice. "Well, thank you very much for your time." I shook the rabbi's hand and we left.

Once outside, Barbara said, "His remarks made a lot of sense, but what he was asking us to undertake seems so overwhelming. I wouldn't even know how to make a start! I have no idea where we go from here."

"That's simple," I said, hoping my tone would cheer her. "We go to the Conservative rabbi — leader of the 'children of truth'!"

THROUGH HIS SECRETARY, I made an appointment with the Conservative rabbi for two o'clock that afternoon. We went there right after lunch. Temple Bnei Emmet was an imposing stone edifice which filled a corner of a residential street and was surrounded by landscaped lawns and topiary.

The rabbi's office, unlike that of his Orthodox counterpart, was a spacious oak-paneled room in the education wing of the building. A number of framed diplomas and certificates were displayed on the wall, the two largest of which were a rabbinic degree from the Jewish Theological Seminary and a doctorate in history from Columbia University. The others were memberships in various societies. The rabbi, Dr. Hirsch, was a tall, distinguished looking man in his mid-fifties with elegantly graying sideburns and matching goatee. We sat in comfortable armchairs while Hsin-Mei was content with the deeply carpeted floor.

Once again, I recounted the story of how I had found Hsin-Mei, and of our interest in converting her to Judaism. The rabbi was quick to respond. "That is really fascinating," he said with enthusiasm. "I've always had an interest in Chinese history. I suppose you know that in Kaifeng, in Mainland China, there was an established community of Chinese Jews. I had the opportunity to inspect a *sefer Torah* from the synagogue in Kaifeng on a recent visit to Cincinnati."

"Yes, Rabbi," I said, "I've read a little about it. The subject is most interesting but, unfortunately, there's hardly a trace left of that community. Perhaps our daughter may help to establish a new line of Chinese Jews...which brings us back to the question of conversion."

"Oh, yes. Well — that is no problem at all. I can easily prepare the necessary documents attesting to your daughter's Jewishness."

Barbara looked perplexed. "Isn't immersion in a *mikveh* a requirement for conversion?" she asked.

"Yes, well, if you want, we can make arrangements to use the swimming pool at the Jewish Community Center."

I could see by Barbara's expression that she was as taken aback as I was. "Is that considered acceptable?"

"There are several opinions that sanction the use of a swimming pool," the rabbi said confidently. "When you are ready to proceed, just contact my secretary. She has a standard form to fill out. If you give her the particulars, I can prepare the documents. There is a modest administrative fee for the service, you understand." We did.

The rabbi went on. "Since you have just arrived in our community, I imagine you have not yet affiliated with any synagogue. We would be happy if you considered Bnei Emmet. I can assure you there are many other professional couples like yourselves who are members, and we are the largest congregation in the city. Miss Goldberg, my secretary, can provide you with membership literature."

"Thank you, Rabbi, " I said. "Am I to understand that conversion of our daughter is simply a matter of your completing certain forms?"

"Yes," the rabbi replied. "As I said, you must first provide some personal background information — for example, your Hebrew name, and that of your father — but it is really not complicated at all. I'm afraid I have another appointment now, but I would welcome an opportunity in the near future to discuss some of your impressions and experiences with Chinese culture in greater depth. Good luck and welcome to our community."

Barbara picked up the membership kit from the secretary. On our way out we peeked into some of the classrooms in the education wing and glanced at the bulletin boards affixed to the walls.

I WAITED UNTIL the drive home to voice my feelings. "A number of things bothered me about this meeting, but most of all the fact that the rabbi made conversion seem so simple, almost like walking through a door. His approach was so casual and superficial. You know, obtaining American citizenship is more complicated. Last week I called the immigration and naturalization service to find out what we need to do for Hsin-Mei. First of all, there's a waiting period of three years. Next we have to provide certain documentation about our own citizenship. Then there's a legal process and a swearing-in ceremony, what an anthropologist would call a cultural *rite de passage* marking transition from one status to another." Barbara was staring out at the passing scenery but I knew she was paying close attention.

"According to this rabbi," I went on, "no such steps are necessary in the conversion process. If becoming a Jew is really as simple as filling out a form, perhaps we should stop worrying about conversion altogether."

"I was bothered by some of the same things," Barbara agreed. "Also that business with the *mikveh* was surprising — a swimming pool just doesn't seem equivalent. Anyway, I'm not ready to stop at this point. You're always telling me we have to first consider all our options, and then make a decision."

"I do say that, don't I."

"Well," Barbara said, "there's one option we haven't considered yet."

"Right you are, " I said, pulling into our driveway. "I'll give them a call and find out if it's still shining."

"What?"

"You remember — 'the light of truth'!"

RABBI KLEIN, the spiritual leader of the Progressive Congregation Ohr Emmet, was very agreeable on the telephone. "Of course, I would be happy to discuss the conversion of your daughter," he said. "We are in the middle of a development campaign. Until we have our own building, we are sharing facilities with the Quaker Church on Forest Avenue. Is it convenient for you and your wife to meet me there on Tuesday afternoon at three?" I assured him it was.

During our meeting, the rabbi listened with interest to my account, then remarked, "I have only had occasion to convert adults in the past. Your daughter's story offers an opportunity we can share with the entire congregation. You mentioned over the phone that you were with us for Rosh Hashanah. You experienced then our approach to worship. We want our members to be involved personally in the service. For the conversion ceremony I would ask you to prepare a presentation in your own words, perhaps including some slides of China together with musical tapes. I would work together with you and refer you to some appropriate Jewish sources, and we could try to find a Hebrew name for your daughter which synthesizes her Chinese and Jewish identities."

"Rabbi Klein, is immersion in a *mikveh* necessary?"

"*I* have never imposed this demand, Mrs. Schwartzbaum. There is also a practical question in gaining access to a *mikveh*, since the group that controls the ritual bath in this city only allows certain individuals to utilize it."

"Which group is that?" I asked.

"The Orthodox congregation."

"Rabbi, permit me to ask if a conversion under your auspices would be generally recognized and accepted?"

Rabbi Klein hesitated a moment before answering Barbara's question. "You should know that many elements in the larger Jewish community will, in fact, choose to ignore this conversion," he said as offhandedly as he could manage. "This is the reality we have to deal with. On the other hand, you must ask yourselves what will provide the most personally meaningful experience, which procedure offers a sense of significance and commitment to the Jewish heritage?"

"Tell me," I challenged, "how do slides of China and musical tapes lead to commitment to Judaism?"

"Judaism," the rabbi pontificated, "requires active intellectual involvement rather than mechanical, reflexive allegiance to antiquated forms. Our approach allows you to integrate the new and the old, contemporary experience and historic memories."

We thanked the rabbi and took our leave. Outside of the wood-frame church, we strolled leisurely to our car, enjoying the bright foliage and the crisp autumn air.

"I'm afraid to ask your impression," Barbara confessed.

"The last time I participated in 'Show and Tell'," I said, "I was in the third grade and I brought a bird's nest that I'd found to class. As I remember, the teacher was very interested but the class was bored. I am no longer in third grade, and Hsin-Mei is not a bird's nest."

Chapter 5

THE NEXT MORNING, before leaving for the university, we reviewed our recent experiences. "I was able to relate to the Orthodox rabbi at a certain level," I said. "He was consistent. There are certain requirements and prerequisites — admissions criteria, if you will — and until these criteria are satisfied, one is not accepted as a Jew."

"There was one major problem," Barbara added. "He didn't describe the criteria clearly or explain how we go about satisfying them. To use your analogy, I don't have any real idea what the admissions fee is, and what we are admitted to after we've paid."

"I agree. You don't simply push a button and become an observant Jew and, in any event, by no stretch of the imagination can I envision our becoming kosher tomorrow or doing all the other things that seem to be required. As for the other rabbis," I continued, "I couldn't relate to them at *all*. They seemed to be operating at such a superficial, shallow intellectual level that I feel it would be meaningless to convert Hsin-Mei in the manner they prescribed. It would just be a pretense, an empty exercise without substance."

"So where does that leave us?"

"Where we were before — two Jewish parents with a

non-Jewish Chinese daughter."

"Well, I can't see anything more we can do at this point either," Barbara agreed. "This whole business has been very frustrating. Still, I have realized one thing from these past few weeks."

"What's that?"

"That I know hardly anything about Judaism. Here we've been running around trying to make our daughter Jewish, when we ourselves don't know the first thing about what it means to *be* a Jew."

THE WEEKS PASSED into months, and the months into years. Our household routine was marked by the rhythm of the seasons, the school calendar, holiday trips and vacations, and visits to and from family. We found time in our busy schedule to regularly read books on Jewish topics and themes. There was no system to our selections, which included fiction, essays, history, polemics, social science, theology and philosophy. While we remained unaffiliated, we attended special events at the Jewish Community Center and local synagogues. Our circle of friends and acquaintances encompassed people from the university and the local Chinese community and our home became an open house for Chinese students studying at nearby universities and colleges.

From time to time, an incident would remind us of Hsin-Mei's anomalous religious status. We were renting our house from a couple who had recently become deeply involved with Pentacostal Fundamentalism. The wife, a daughter of an Episcopal bishop, and the husband, a successful businessman, were now "true believers" in an evangelical Protestant faith. Their recent involvement and commitment was so total that they fervently believed that part of their mission was to convince others to follow their "genuine path."

Since the rental agreement, together with a three-month

deposit, had been arranged prior to our departure from Taiwan, we had not personally met our landlords until several months after our arrival. The owners, upon discovering that their tenants were two Jews with a yet undefined Chinese baby, were sure that they had received some heavenly sign. When they also realized that the house was regularly visited by large numbers of Asian students, the majority of whom were Buddhist, they were absolutely convinced that they had acquired a divine mission.

Barbara and I, through a combination of polite sternness and total disinterest, finally managed to deflect their evangelical overtures. And while we found the whole affair amusing, we also found it disturbing. It was one more reminder of Hsin-Mei's marginal situation and our own limited knowledge — we were frequently unable to counter adequately the barrage of religious arguments directed at us.

I'M THE KIND OF PERSON who is usually content to let things drift, but my sociological and political curiosity impelled me to make periodic inquiries regarding the broader aspects of the conversion issue. On one occasion, I spoke to the principal of the city's Hebrew Day School, where a full-day educational program from kindergarten to eighth grade was offered. The more we studied, the more we saw how ignorant we were about our own religion, so it seemed like a good idea for our daughter to have the benefit of at least a basic Jewish education.

I informed the Day School principal of my family's situation and inquired about Hsin-Mei's future enrollment eligibility. The principal advised me that only Jewish children could be admitted. I pressed him for his definition of "Jewish", and the principal explained that this meant "according to the rules of Jewish law or *halachah*."

"What does this mean with respect to conversion?" I asked, and received the answer I'd expected: conversion under Orthodox auspices.

After our first year in the community, the local Jewish Federation discovered our existence and we were contacted during every fundraising effort. By examining the information packet which accompanied each solicitation, I learned that the Day School was one of the recipients of funds collected in the annual campaign. A careful reading of the fine print disclosed that over forty percent of the total operating costs of the school was acquired through this channel, the remainder being obtained through tuition and other fundraising efforts. I thought I'd discovered the chink in Orthodoxy's armor. I quickly called the local Jewish Federation and made an appointment to see the director.

At the time of the interview, I introduced myself and explained that my wife and I were relative newcomers to the community. I casually mentioned something about our background and my position with the university before raising the real point of my visit. "It is my understanding that the current fundraising drive is a community endeavor which includes unaffiliated individuals as well as members of all the various synagogues."

The director, a bald, bespectacled little man in his late fifties, agreed emphatically. "Absolutely! In fact as you probably noticed, the theme for this year's campaign is 'We are One'. We are united not only with our fellow Jews in Israel, but also in serving as many needs of the local Jewish community as we are able to."

"I'm glad to hear that," I said. "Then if, as a member of the local Jewish community, I require some assistance, and a facility exists for providing that service, I should be able to avail myself of that service. Is that correct?"

"Of course," the director answered, suddenly wary. He was a bit puzzled by the direction the discussion was taking. "But I'm sure you appreciate that individuals also have a responsibility. That is the whole basis of the campaign. We ask everyone to contribute so that when a need arises, they themselves, as well as others, will have a place to go to."

"But what if one fulfills his responsibility and then, upon seeking assistance from a Jewish agency, is denied access to that assistance?" The director was now on his guard. "I'm not sure what you're driving at. Can you explain what you mean?"

"I am referring to the Hebrew Day School. I noticed in the campaign literature that the school is listed as a constituent institution of the Jewish community, and that a percentage of the monies which are collected go to support the school. In fact, these funds comprise a significant portion of the school's overall budget. Yet, if I wished to enroll my daughter in that school, she would not be accepted."

The director was genuinely surprised. "What do you mean?" he asked.

"Unless my daughter was converted in a particular manner," I said, "a manner not subscribed to by the majority of the rabbis in this community, she would be ineligible to enroll. Yet the school is listed as a community institution."

He moved uneasily in his chair and ran a hand over his bald pate. "I will try to explain this situation. While organizations and agencies affiliate with the larger Jewish community and participate in the annual campaign, they still remain independent units with their own boards of directors and by-laws. Each unit retains considerable autonomy. For example, Jewish Family Services, which handles the majority of the social service needs of the community, has its own criteria for eligibility. In addition, almost every unit is affiliated with other organizations. The Jewish Community Center and Jewish Family Services participate in the city-wide United Givers Fund and derive financial assistance from this source. As a result they must follow certain guidelines set down by this organization."

"Such as?"

"Well, the United Fund has certain regulations regarding non-discrimination in the delivery of services."

"That may explain something I found quite curious," I

interjected. "I was looking at the Jewish Community Center's membership rolls the other day, and it appeared — on the basis of last names and addresses — that close to half of the membership is comprised of non-Jews."

"Yes, that's true. This is also partially explained by the fact that the membership fees at the Community Center are lower than the YMCA, for example."

"The outcome seems paradoxical," I observed somewhat sarcastically. "One constituent organization develops a set of policies which attracts non-Jews and another organization does all it can to keep Jews out, or, should I say, certain *types* of Jews."

"I can understand your feelings," the director said with a sigh, "but, I don't think you are being entirely fair or objective. The Day School, like most of our constituent organizations, is affiliated with its own parent body — in this case an Orthodox one — and must follow its principles and guidelines."

I felt a sudden pang of sympathy for this little beaten-down administrator. The web of creases and wrinkles that crisscrossed his cheeks and brow were the battle scars of a career-clerk who'd long since given up the struggle. His only mission now was to hold the organization line until he reached retirement age. His days of fighting injustice were behind him.

"Am I the first person to raise this issue about the Day School?" I asked, abandoning my aggressive tone.

"It has come up before," the director replied. "Unfortunately some individuals have actually withheld their contributions because of it. Now, if you'll excuse me, I have a meeting which I must attend." He rose and stretched out his hand. "Before we conclude, let me encourage you to become active in the Federation. We're a volunteer organization and if you have concerns, the only effective way to express them is by working with others in developing and implementing policy."

THAT EVENING, when I told Barbara what had transpired, she said, "I don't really understand why you went there in the first place. He couldn't have done anything that would alter our own personal situation. What did you hope to achieve?"

"You're right. I've been asking myself the same question ever since I left the director's office this morning. I guess I'm just trying to better understand how the system works. It's become increasingly clear to me that we're not operating in a religious framework, but rather in a political and economic one, and a complex one at that."

"You know, I really think that's exactly your problem," Barbara chided. "You want to reduce everything in this world to some form of political or social reality based on such things as influence and money. But every time I look at Hsin-Mei and think about how she came into our lives, I realize that we in fact control very little."

"I'm not sure what you're trying to say."

"Let me put it this way. From the time you found Hsin-Mei, through all the problems in bringing her to America and all the business with the conversion, up to and including today's episode, you have never yet used one particularly essential word."

"Which word is that?" I asked.

"God."

◁

*I walked down this path
each day from the
faculty compound to the
village of Tamsui.*

*The fishermen's families
live on the fishing boats
and sleep belowdecks at
night.*

▽

△

Lung-Shan is the most famous temple in Taiwan.

A hilltop guesthouse (note staircase) similar to the Okinawa inn we visited. The view from the crest is worth the climb. ▷

In Taiwan, Barbara learned to play the gunchung (a sort of zither) and I studied the diza (a bamboo flute).

Barbara took second place in the Chinese language competition for foreign residents.

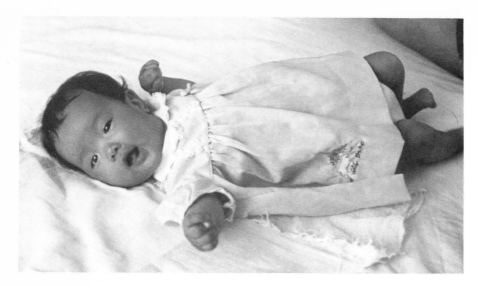

Our neighbors generously provided "Hsin-Mei" with a layette, including this hand-embroidered dress.

Mei-Mei and five of her children. Her oldest daughter (second from left) occasionally helped out with the cooking and food shopping.

1

兹有中華民國國民

前往 美國(以下空白)

應請友邦民政及軍事機關准予自由通行並請必要時予

中華民國駐

年 月 號

翁玉

3

Description

福 貫 福建 省 者 林森 縣/市

出生日期
Date of Birth   MAY 6, 1972

出生地點
Place of Birth   CHINA

身高
Height   公尺 m. 44 公分 c.m. or   呎 ft.   吋 in.

職業
Occupation

婚姻狀況
Marital Status   SINGLE

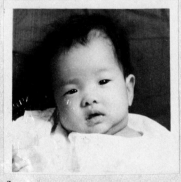

簽名
            (Signature of bearer)

2

The Ministry of Foreign Affairs of the Republic of China requests all civil and military authorities of Friendly States to let pass freely

Miss WEN, Yu - Ping
alias KIM DAVRA SCHWARTZBAUM

a national of the Republic of China, going to

U.S.A. VIA ALL NECESSARY COUNTRIES EN ROUTE (LEAVING BLANK)

and afford assistance and protection in case of necessity.

For the Minister
and by Authorization

PASSPORT SECTION
Consular Affairs Department

4

外交部 (61)人 字第065371 號
中華民國 61 年 7 月 7 日簽發

持照人在本護照有效期間內准予進入中華民國台灣省。

MINISTRY OF FOREIGN AFFAIRS
REPUBLIC OF CHINA

Date: JUL - 7 1972

The bearer/s of this passport is/are permitted to enter the Province of Taiwan, Republic of China, if this passport remains valid.

By authorization

85

▽ *Yu-Bing — Hsin-Mei — Kim Davra became Devorah after her conversion but her impish smile and cheerful nature remained unchanged.*

△ *Mei-Mei and Dovie took to one another immediately.*

◁ *"Hsin-Mei" and a friend on Chinese New Year (note banners around doorway inscribed with New Year greetings).*

Each morning the hundreds of kindergarteners in Devorah's school started the day with calisthenics.

Blonde, blue-eyed Dov Chaim attracted a lot of attention when he visited his sister's school.

"Toiveling" our new dishes in the China Sea prompted Mei-Mei to coin the aphorism: "The pot that knows the ocean will cook the fish, the dish that tastes the sea will serve it."

One of my students and her family were among the many guests we entertained in our bamboo sukkah.
▽

BEFORE WE HAD traveled to Taiwan, during our year-long stay there, and for more than two years after our return, Barbara had been seeking professional advice and assistance regarding fertility and conception. Examinations of both of us revealed no medical reason for our inability to have children. After visiting yet another specialist, Barbara announced, "I'm tired of all these appointments and prescriptions. I'm just going to let the situation ride for now."

"There doesn't seem to be anything else we can do."

"There *is* one thing we haven't seriously tried yet," Barbara said as she cleared the supper table.

"What's that?" I asked.

She looked into my eyes for a moment before she answered simply: "Prayer."

SOMETIME AFTER Hsin-Mei's second birthday, we decided to investigate the possibility of a second adoption and made an appointment with the head of Jewish Family Services. She was a pale, square, middle-aged woman who seemed to be built into her desk. She moved heavily behind a barrier of files and carried on her face a cultivated expression of concern. Her telephone cord curled around her office like a life-support system and indeed she seemed to draw on it frequently as she answered every one of the many calls that interrupted our interview.

She was very understanding and sympathetic. She first referred to the existing demographic and social situation which accounted for the shrinking pool of adoptive children. Then she explained that legal abortions, together with the greater social acceptability of raising children born out of wedlock, had resulted in fewer and fewer children being available each year. She indicated that placements were more likely if a couple were willing to consider special categories, such as older children or those with various physical and mental handicaps.

"In short, you have no babies to offer us."

She gave me a stiff smile. "Jewish Family Services cooperates with our sister agencies, such as Catholic Charities, in order to locate suitable candidates for adoption."

I inquired whether these other organizations objected to children they helped place being converted to Judaism.

"But you are both Jewish," she replied. "Why is conversion necessary?"

I looked at her incredulously. "You mean you didn't realize that if a Jewish couple adopts a non-Jewish child, the child has to be converted in order to become Jewish?"

"Well, the matter never came up in any previous placements we helped arrange," she assured us. "But, if you are correct, I wouldn't anticipate any problems."

"It's not so simple," I said. "Are you aware of the fact that unless the child has an Orthodox conversion, he or she is not eligible to enroll in the Hebrew Day School?"

"Are you sure of this? I find that hard to believe." One eyebrow rose imperiously on her forehead.

"I suggest you call the Federation or the Day School for confirmation."

"If you don't mind, I will do just that." She chose to do "just that" from an adjoining office — perhaps her life-support phone was only for incoming calls — and returned five minutes later. "You were correct," she reported without apology. "I must say I find this situation shocking and most disconcerting."

"I'm afraid I don't understand," said Barbara, surprised at the intensity of the social worker's reaction. "Jewish Family Services assists Jewish families. Isn't it natural that requirements of Jewish law be followed when necessary?"

"Of course," the woman replied, "but not when these requirements interfere with individual freedom and the unimpeded growth and development of the client." It was an affront to her sense of bureaucratic pride.

On the way out of the office, I told Barbara, "The more I find out about this community, the more it becomes clear to me that it isn't a single community but rather a number of little enclaves, each operating according to its own philosophy and set of rules."

"I'm not sure why we even came today," Barbara said. "How can we consider adopting another gentile child when Hsin-Mei is almost two-and-a-half and she *still* isn't Jewish?"

HSIN-MEI WAS a vivacious, pigtailed three-year-old with straight dark bangs, dimples and dancing eyes. Shortly before her birthday, she received a registered letter stating that her application for United States naturalization had been approved, and on the appointed day we brought her to the Federal Courthouse for the swearing-in ceremony.

The designated courtroom was crowded with new citizens and their families, and the ceremony was serious, dignified and moving, as befitted an occasion of such import. The presiding judge read out the names of the new citizens and their countries of origin — Italy, Vietnam, Ireland, Venezuela, Mexico, the Philippines, China — forty-five individuals altogether, representing twenty-one countries. Hsin-Mei was the youngest and — need I say? — cutest participant. The judge delivered a brief speech after which the assembly recited the oath of allegiance. Hsin-Mei, along with the others, received a letter which read in part:

Dear Fellow Citizen:
There are certain unforgettable moments in everyone's life — moments that we treasure as long as we live. I hope that for you this is one of them. It is my pleasure to welcome you most warmly to citizenship of the United States of America.

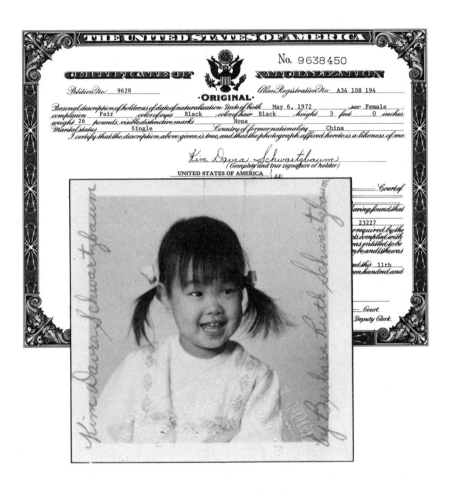

THE UNITED STATES OF AMERICA

No. 9638450

CERTIFICATE OF NATURALIZATION

Petition No. 9628   *Alien Registration No.* A34 108 194

·ORIGINAL·

Personal description of holder as of date of naturalization· Date of birth May 6, 1972   *sex* Female; *complexion* Fair   *color of eyes* Black   *color of hair* Black   *height* 3 *feet* 0 *inches;* *weight* 26 *pounds; visible distinctive marks* None *Marital status* Single   *Country of former nationality* China

I certify that the description above given is true, and that the photograph affixed hereto is a likeness of me.

Kim Davra Schwartzbaum
(Complete and true signature of holder)

UNITED STATES OF AMERICA } ss:

"Kim Davra"'s U.S. Naturalization Certificate.

The message was signed by Gerald R. Ford. Barbara and I had decided that as part of the naturalization process it would be appropriate to give Hsin-Mei a more American name. The certificate of naturalization we received after the ceremony stated that "Kim Davra Schwartzbaum, alien registration number A34-109-194, born in China, May 6, 1972, height 3 feet, weight 26 pounds, single, black eyes, black hair, on March 11, 1975 has in all respects complied with the applicable provisions of the naturalization laws and is entitled to be admitted to citizenship.'' We had chosen the popular American name, Kim, for its oriental flavor, and Davra for my late father, David.

EVER SINCE HER RETURN to the United States, Barbara had been eager to renew her Chinese studies. She had been working with a tutor and learning at home, but she felt that this approach was less than satisfactory. The nearest graduate program in Chinese, however, was at Georgetown University, more than two hours' drive from our area. Despite the logistics problem, Barbara applied and was accepted as a candidate for a Master of Arts in Chinese Language and Linguistics.

Barbara managed to arrange a school schedule that enabled her to be away from home only two days a week. A Chinese family agreed to care for Hsin-Mei on those days and I picked her up from their house after work, prepared our supper, and put her to sleep at night.

Since her classes were on two consecutive days, it made sense for Barbara to stay over in Washington, but she had considerable difficulty in finding suitable lodging. A classmate suggested she inquire at one of the local convents, and as a result Barbara became a part-time sojourner in the community of the Sisters of the Visitation. I joked about the arrangement and Barbara's "cloistered life," but privately I felt relieved that she was able to stay in a secure and convenient facility.

Barbara loved her studies but missed us very much, even for the short time that she was away. Late in the afternoon after classes, she would return alone to her small chamber in the convent, walking past the religious icons present on each floor. The figures seemed cold and foreign. She would quickly enter her room and shut the door firmly behind her.

ONCE A WEEK I would drop in at the campus Hillel House. It was a structure similar to the various sorority and fraternity houses that dotted the grounds of the university, and was a place where the Jewish students gathered to relax or study. I often brought a sandwich and read the publications and periodicals available in the lounge there.

One afternoon, I glanced up from the magazine I was reading and noticed a man I hadn't seen on campus before. He was bearded and wore a dark suit and hat. He approached me and, stretching out his hand, said, "How do you do? I'm Rabbi Joseph Goldstein. I'm the new principal of the Hebrew Day School." I shook his hand and introduced myself. "I was in this part of the city," he said, "and thought I'd stop in and see what the Hillel House was like. No one seems to be here except you."

"Yes, it's usually quiet like this. A few students live upstairs, but from what I've observed, there isn't a great deal of student interest in the facility."

"Have you lived in this community long?" the rabbi asked. "You'll pardon me for saying so, but your accent doesn't sound local."

I laughed and told him that I was from New York and that I had a wife and a three-year-old daughter. We chatted easily for a while, each of us newcomers trying to make the most of our chance encounter. But all too soon, it was time for both of us to go our separate ways.

"It would be my pleasure," said the rabbi, "if you and your family would join us for Shabbos."

"I'm afraid we probably live too far from you to join you for Shabbos," I said, touched at his spontaneous offer. "We're on the north side. I presume you live in the west end, nearer the synagogues and the Day School."

"That's right," Rabbi Goldstein said, "but that's no problem — you'll sleep over in our home on Friday night."

"Thank you very much," I said. "Let me speak to my wife and I'll call you by tomorrow morning."

Barbara was very enthusiastic. I phoned the rabbi that evening and accepted his gracious invitation.

WE HAD NO TROUBLE following the rabbi's precise directions and arrived at the Goldstein home forty-five minutes before the onset of the Sabbath. The house was bustling with activity. Mrs. Goldstein was busy attending to last-minute preparations, so the rabbi showed us to our room. He announced that he and his oldest son would be leaving for Friday night services in a few minutes. I got my family settled and joined the Goldsteins for the ten-minute walk through the quiet residential neighborhood.

On the way, I remarked that this would be my second visit to Shaarei Emmet and briefly recounted my earlier meeting with the congregational rabbi. Rabbi Goldstein listened with interest. "You know," he said, "the synagogue has a new rabbi. I think you'll enjoy meeting him."

A group of about fifteen men were assembled in the sanctuary when we entered and *minchah*, the afternoon service, commenced immediately. Rabbi Goldstein helped me find the proper place in the prayer book. I was pleased to discover that I could still read the vowelized Hebrew, but it was slow going.

During the break between the afternoon prayers and the service for welcoming the Sabbath, the new rabbi, a young man of about twenty-eight, introduced himself as Rabbi Israel Kaufman. He was outgoing, friendly and almost a bit too eager, which I attributed to his relative youth and the earnestness associated with a new position.

With the assistance of Rabbi Goldstein, I was able to follow most of the remaining service. I was a bit surprised at how comfortable and at ease I felt at Shaarei Emmet, perhaps because the congregation was small and the sanctuary close and intimate. It could have been the warmth of the new rabbi; possibly it was the chanting of the prayers and the occasional singing, which created a composed and peaceful mood. But I felt it was something deeper — a distant echo of something past.

After the service, the congregants wished each other "Good Shabbos." The rabbi and I walked back in silence. The air was crisp and sharp, the night sky dark, the streets quiet and dim. As Rabbi Goldstein opened his front door, the flames of the Sabbath candles flared and the dining room was filled with light.

FROM THAT TIME ON, we spent one Shabbos every month as guests of one of the Orthodox families in the community. With each visit, we learned some new practice, idea or inspiring thought which we then incorporated into our own celebrations of the Sabbath. Slowly, imperceptibly, our observance grew and developed. Barbara now lit candles regularly and I started to recite *kiddush* over the wine. On clear days, I walked the three-and-a-half miles to the synagogue on Saturday and returned home reinforced by the modest collation provided by the shul. Barbara even baked her own *challos* and our Saturday meals began to take on a more relaxed, festive flavor. We found ourselves substituting our Saturday afternoon drives with long, aimless strolls around the neighborhood. The Sabbath became the high point of our week, a time which we anticipated and looked forward to.

One day, I heard that a new rabbi had joined the community, a rabbi who had been ordained at Yeshiva University. The fact that he'd accepted a position with a suburban congregation, the majority of whose members were not fully observant, was of particular interest to me. "They say this rabbi is quite open in his outlook," I told Barbara.

"What does *that* mean?" she asked. "Don't forget those other rabbis we talked to — they were so open that everything worthwhile seemed to have escaped."

"What I mean is that while he's an Orthodox rabbi, he's had more experience dealing with non-religious people. And he's also college-educated. I'd like to discuss Hsin-Mei with him."

"Okay," she said without enthusiasm, "if you feel it will be useful." Despite her dubiousness, Barbara agreed to go with me to see him.

RABBI FRIED'S STYLE was very informal. After we reviewed our previous discussions regarding conversion and described our current level of observance, he got right to the point. "As far as I'm concerned, there are four mandatory criteria: you must keep the Sabbath, you must follow the laws of *kashrus*, you must observe the requirements of family purity in your married life, and you must agree to provide your daughter with the best Jewish education available in the community — which means, at this time, enrollment in the Hebrew Day School."

"What about all the other six hundred-plus *mitzvos* in the Torah?" I asked.

"In religious observance, each of us is on a ladder," the rabbi replied. "What matters is the direction in which we are climbing. If you commit yourselves to these four criteria, you will see that the other *mitzvos* begin to follow in their wake. *Shabbos, kashrus, taharas ha-mishpachah* — the laws of family purity — are like powerful magnets. Once you observe them, they will pull the other *mitzvos* into your life."

Barbara asked if he meant we had to keep kosher both in and out of our home.

"Someone once asked me that same question," replied the rabbi. "What I told her was that if you keep kosher only in your home, then your dishes will go to heaven." We laughed at his joke. "Really, I don't mean to be cute, but you have to understand that Judaism is a seamless web. There are no easy escape hatches. Kosher is kosher, non-kosher food is non-kosher food, and whether it is eaten in your home or outside, it still goes into your body."

"Well, Rabbi Fried," Barbara declared, "I for one am ready to take on these requirements. For the past year, we've been becoming more and more Sabbath-observant. Both Allan and I are vegetarians, so I really don't see any great difficulty in making our home completely kosher. We've been anxious to have Hsin-Mei enroll in the Hebrew Day School since our arrival — the problem has not been with us, but with her ineligibility. And as far as family purity is concerned, I'm afraid I'm not very knowledgeable about these laws, but I'm prepared to study and learn about them."

"What about yourself?" Rabbi Fried asked me.

"Barbara's response pretty much represents my own views," I said.

"Well, we're in business," said the rabbi. He handed us several books dealing with *taharas ha-mishpachah*. "Please read these carefully and write down any questions you have so we can discuss them later. Next, I would like to set a time when I can visit your home so we can see exactly what has to be done to *kasher* your kitchen and utensils. Finally, if you're free tomorrow evening, I'd like you to meet me at the local supermarket. We can walk through the aisles together and I can point out the various categories of kosher food and the different symbols used to distinguish kosher products."

Barbara was very excited on our way home from the meeting. So was I. "For the first time we have a concrete set of guidelines," I said. "This rabbi was able to be specific. I'm not sure exactly what's involved with each of his require-ments, but at least what he's asking of us is delimited and defined, not open-ended, vague and ambiguous as it was with the first Orthodox rabbi we talked to. I like this approach much better than abstract, philosophical principles."

We devoted ourselves to the agenda that Rabbi Fried had set for us. Gradually our home became completely kosher, although we encountered a number of technical problems along the way. In the end, we decided to acquire all new dishes. The rabbi helped us overcome the problems associated with *kasher*ing our dishwasher, but he determined that it was not possible to *kasher* the rubber racks. Fortunately we were able to find replacements.

BARBARA AND I approached these activities in very different ways. I, with my behavioral science training, was analytical. I tried to understand how the requirements of Jewish law served individual and group functions. I explained to Barbara how keeping kosher acted to limit one's circle of friends to other observant Jews. "If you invite someone to your home," I said, "food is an inevitable social necessity. It serves as a social lubricant facilitating interaction and sociability. Obviously if someone invites you to *his* home, you will eventually want to reciprocate, since social relations are based on the maintenance of some crude balance of rewards. Now, if you can't reciprocate by inviting a couple who entertained you in *their* home, to *your* home, because they won't eat your food since it is ritually unfit, that places a strain on the relationship and, all things being equal, the relationship will eventually attenuate. This then contributes to a limiting of social contacts to one's own in-group and ultimately promotes an endogamous marriage system."

Barbara, who was busy sorting laundry during my profound lecture, remarked without looking up, "That's all very well and good, especially from someone who doesn't like abstract principles and prefers concrete, specific instructions. What counts in the final analysis is that we're supposed to keep kosher because we're commanded to do so, and as far as I'm concerned, it introduces an added dimension to one's meals. Food is no longer something which one prepares, but it becomes part of a larger sphere of spirituality."

We saw the *mikveh* for the first time when we brought all our new dishes and utensils for immersion in the ritual bath.

With its pastel-tiled walls and submerged flight of stairs, it looked like an indoor swimming pool that had been cut down in its youth. The dimensions were those of a large bath but its depth suggested a deep pond with clear water rising to the topmost edge. As I lowered our glassware and plates and pots into the pool, the face I saw reflected in the surface was serious and intense, but my heart was light with the knowledge that this was one more positive step in the right direction.

Having committed ourselves, we were determined to comply with all that Rabbi Fried had asked of us, but the next step was far more difficult than the preceding ones. It involved a drastic change in our lifestyle and a constant awareness of things to which we previously had never given much attention.

We were fascinated to find that the ancient laws of "family purity" conformed so logically to natural biological rhythms and that Jewish sages of nearly two millennia ago had been so well-informed in matters that the modern medical profession was only beginning to comprehend. A set of laws which called for deferred gratification, self-discipline, and mutual trust and understanding stood in sharp contrast to the "new morality" — the frenetic search for pleasure that prevailed in secular society of the era.

Because of our years of fertility treatment, the concept of intervals of abstention was not new to us, but refraining totally from all physical contact was. It compelled us to learn to communicate in other, permissible ways and this actually seemed to enrich our relationship. Several evenings a week, Barbara studied with Rabbi Fried's wife and she soon came to terms with the regulations governing "modesty" and covering her hair.

When we looked back on the preceding weeks and the transformation our life had undergone, we could not help but be amazed. We had not embarked on this undertaking with the express intent of becoming Orthodox Jews, but in fact we had, and it felt wonderful. We believed in everything we were doing and our faith in God became stronger with each additional *mitzvah* we observed.

FOUR MONTHS LATER, Rabbi Fried agreed to organize a religious court for Hsin-Mei's conversion. The principal of the Day School — Rabbi Goldstein, Rabbi Kaufman of the Orthodox synagogue, and Rabbi Fried constituted the *beis din*. They concluded that it would be permissible for me to go into the *mikveh* with Hsin-Mei in order to ensure that she was completely submerged for the required three times and to avoid any danger, since the depth of the water in the *mikveh* exceeded her height.

Hsin-Mei disrobed. I held her hand gently. Together we walked slowly down the steps into the *mikveh*. I could feel that she was tense and unsure. The water on the steps was warm around our bare feet.

I entered first, then reached over and lifted Hsin-Mei into my arms. "Listen, honey," I said, "you are going to dunk yourself three times. There is nothing to be afraid of. I'll be with you all the time." Hsin-Mei's eyes were trusting.

I released her and she slipped from my arms. The waters of the *mikveh* embraced her. Twice again I held and relinquished my daughter. As I glanced up, I saw the three rabbis, their faces solemn.

Later, as Barbara, Hsin-Mei and I were leaving the *mikveh* building, Rabbi Fried wished us "Mazel Tov" and handed me an official letter. The English translation read:

> *We attest that the young girl, Devorah, daughter of Avraham Avinu, was immersed in a kosher mikveh: We now welcome her as our own daughter and declare to her, "Blessed God, the father of Avraham our father, guide her that she may follow and walk in your path. Amen." And for this purpose we came together as a beis din in the city designated below and witness this conversion with*

our signature today, Wednesday, the 12th day of the
month of Iyar 5736.

The next morning, Barbara read from the *siddur*:
My God,
The soul you have placed in me
Is pure.
You it was Who created it,
You formed it,
You breathed it into me,
You guard it within me,
You will take it from me,
And return it to me, in time-to-be.

All the time the soul is within me
I give thanks before Thee,
O Lord, my God and God of my fathers,
Master of all works,
Lord of all the souls.

She closed the *siddur* and reached over to Devorah and held
her in her arms.

Ten days later, on the 22nd of Iyar, Devorah turned four years
old.

Eleven months later, on the 26th of Nissan 5737, Barbara
gave birth to Dov Chaim.

THERE IS NO DOUBT in my mind that the apparent miracle of Dov Chaim's birth, after twelve years of childlessness, was a direct outcome of my discovery of Devorah. Had I not found her, it is probable that Barbara and I would have continued as we were until the end of our days, because the fact is that we were not dissatisfied with our existence, we were not searching for our identity, we did not feel unfulfilled, except with respect to raising a family. But had we adopted a Jewish baby instead of a Chinese one, it is doubtful that we would have embarked on the long road to find our heritage.

However, when that tiny bundle unexpectedly came into our lives, events began to progress with their own momentum. Our desire to "merely" convert the baby to Judaism compelled us to take our first tentative steps toward Torah observance. And just as Rabbi Fried had predicted, our fulfillment of the three most basic *mitzvos* led inevitably to our fulfillment of many others as well. Thus I found myself, eight days after the birth of our *bechor*, performing the *mitzvah* of *bris milah*.

Our newborn son, our first *bris* — the excitement was intoxicating. The *bris* was held at Shaarei Emmet and as the *mohel* bent over his charge I recited the words I had so long dreamed of reciting: "Behold I am prepared and ready to perform the positive commandment that the Creator, blessed is He, has commanded me to circumcise my son." The baby lay innocent and unsuspecting across the *sandak*'s knees with the *mohel* hovering above. In an instant it was done and the *mohel*, accompanied by Dov Chaim's hearty wail, exclaimed triumphantly, "Just as he has entered into the Covenant, so may he enter into Torah, into marriage and into good deeds." I was òvercome by the magnitude of the moment and could barely compose myself for the task ahead — my speech.

Barbara cradled a sleeping Dov Chaim while I mounted the podium to deliver the words that had come to me while I had nervously awaited his arrival. My theme was the *berachos* which are recited each morning, for as I contemplated the birth of our firstborn they took on a new meaning. I saw in these blessings my son's future, the entire life cycle of a Jew.

" 'Blessed are You, *Hashem*,' " I began, " 'Who gave the rooster understanding to distinguish between day and night.' The rooster is endowed with a special sensitivity to dawn, to the rays of the sun and minute quantities of light we humans cannot detect. The precision of timing is one of *Hashem*'s gifts to the world. It was this innate timing that signaled the onset of the birth process which distinguished between day — the new life of our son — and the night that preceded it.

" 'Blessed are You, *Hashem*,' " I went on, " 'Who gives sight to the blind...Who clothes the naked...Who releases the imprisoned.' Our son came into this world unseeing, naked, and shackled to his mother. In moments, he could see and his nakedness was covered. His birth released a new life, a new servant of *Hashem*. The Hebrew word for the imprisoned, אסורים, contains a *samech*, a letter totally confined, sealed off. Release the *samech* and אורים, lights, remains — the light brought into our life by our new son and the light of Torah.

"'Who straightens the bent.' For nine months our developing son remained bent inside his mother. כפופים has two *fehs*, a letter which represents the fetal position. They are separated by a straight *vav* which represents our hopes for how he will grow.

"'Who spreads out the earth upon the waters.' We pray to *Hashem* that our son will grow and mature, that he will have the stability and firmness of earth that only a Jewish education and upbringing can provide.

"'Who provided me with all my needs.' What, indeed, did I lack in my life but to have children of my own? This, too, *Hashem* has provided.

"'Who prepares the steps of man.' We pray our son will grow to be independent and self-reliant, to stand on his own two feet.

"'Who girds Israel with might.' May *Hashem* grant Dov Chaim the ability to reach the strength of early manhood of which it is written: 'The glory of young men is their strength' (*Mishlei* 20:29).

"'Who crowns Israel with glory.' It is written, 'Fullness of years is a crown of glory' (*Mishlei* 16:31). May *Hashem* allow the privilege of long life to Dov Chaim and may he be blessed with children and grandchildren, for it is also written, 'Children's children are the crown of old men' (*Mishlei* 17:6).

"'Who gives strength to the weary.' And may Dov Chaim and all of us gathered here have the strength to see our later years ones of happiness and fulfillment and may we only come together as today for festive occasions and *mitzvos* performed with joy."

THE WEEKS THAT FOLLOWED were a whirlwind of diapers, middle-of-the-night feedings, and relearning the infant routines we had "enjoyed" with Devorah four years earlier. But all this took second place to the very special occasion on the horizon, an occasion which virtually filled us with awe — our son's *pidyon ha-ben.*

Everything that opens the womb, that must be presented to God, among man and beast, shall be yours; however, the firstborn son of man you must redeem... The redemption from one month of age shall be according to your value, five shekels of silver...(Numbers 18:15-16). "Everything that opens the womb," the Torah states. A child born following an earlier miscarriage or a child delivered by caesarean section or an adopted child are therefore exempt. Dov Chaim most definitely qualified for "redemption".

The ceremony took place in the synagogue, and it was my obligation to transfer the equivalent of five shekels of silver to a *Kohain* in order to redeem, or reclaim, my son. Barbara brought Dovie in on an ornate silver tray decorated with sweets and jewelry, and handed it to me. I placed the tray before the *Kohain* and he asked: "Which do you prefer — to give me your firstborn or to redeem him for five silver coins?"

I provided the designated response: "I prefer to redeem my son and here is his redemption money as I am bound to do according to the law of Torah." Dovie was unmoved, but for Barbara and me this was a very special moment. I spoke later at the *seudas mitzvah.*

"Every *mitzvah* we perform," I said, "takes place only because we are first granted a gift by *Hashem.* It is this gift which enables us to do the *mitzvah.* To say a blessing over bread first requires bread; to say a *berachah* before reading the Torah requires the greatest gift of all, the holy Torah. So, today, when I recited the benediction 'Blessed are You, Lord, Who has bidden us to redeem the firstborn son,' I first needed a son. Without a gift from *Hashem* — in this case, a firstborn son — it would have been impossible for me to fulfill the *mitzvah* of *pidyon ha-ben.*

"Yet, as we strive to carry out our obligations as Jews," I continued, "we often forget the gifts that preceded our *mitz-*

vos. Today that is impossible. Today one cannot but see the extent of *Hashem*'s *chessed*. The *pasuk* says, 'Everything that opens the womb,' indicating that this opening is not automatic; it is a gift, a *nes*, just as the opening of the Red Sea was for Moshe and *bnei Yisrael*; just as the opening of the Jordan River was for Yehoshua and the Children of Israel on their way to *Eretz Yisrael*."

Dov Chaim at three years.

In this, my second attempt at a genuine *dvar Torah*, I spoke of problems of conception and childbirth based on a *Chazal* on Vashti from the text of *Megillas Esther*, and concluded by connecting this to the *berachah*, "Blessed are You, *Hashem*, Who heals all flesh." "Four years ago," I said, "*Hashem* brought into this world a tiny Chinese baby. When she reached the age of one month, we celebrated the event in China in a ceremony acknowledging that her viability and health had been established. The ceremony was little more than mimicry of the customs of our hosts, for we were never anything but strangers in their land and we certainly never accepted their religion as our own. We could not have known then where that Chinese child would lead us.

"Now, this same child is Jewish, and less than a year after she became a part of *klal Yisrael*, our firstborn son — born twelve years after we were married — reached the age of one month. Today our celebration is steeped in meaning. Today I stood before you bearing the yoke of the kingdom of Heaven and redeemed my son from the *Kohain* as the Torah commanded me.

"Blessed are You, *Hashem*, Who heals all flesh and performs wonders!"

PART THREE:

sunrise

If I take the wings of the sunrise
[in the east] and dwell
in the uttermost parts of the west,
even there shall Your hand lead
me, and Your right hand hold me.

PSALMS 139:9-10

Chapter 1

I N MAY OF 1977, I received a telegram notifying me that I had been awarded a second Fulbright Fellowship to China. Both Barbara and I were very excited at the prospect of returning to Taiwan. For Barbara, it meant that she could more conveniently pursue her Chinese studies; and for me, that I could carry out my plans for a research project on industrial development. In addition, we were most anxious to be reunited with our many close friends in China. But after our initial burst of enthusiasm, we realized that we had less than two months to attend to all the details.

One evening, during a break from packing, Barbara raised an important question. "Do you think we'll encounter any problems with being observant when we get back to Taiwan?"

I thought about it for a moment. "I don't think so," I said. "As far as *kashrus* is concerned, we simply won't eat any meat for the entire year — that shouldn't be hard for vegetarians like ourselves. We can get fish that are kosher fresh from the market and clean them ourselves. And Shabbos is really up to us — I don't see any problems there."

"But, Allan, what will we do about a *mikveh*?"

"Now *that* may be a problem!" In all the hustle and bustle and excitement surrounding our trip, we had inadvertently lost sight of the things that had become so important to us! For a few seconds I actually thought about canceling, then I remembered something I had read. "In one of the books Rabbi Fried gave us on family purity," I told Barbara, "it said that any free-flowing body of water, like a river or lake, can serve as a *mikveh*."

"You're right!" Barbara exclaimed. "But what body of water did you have in mind?"

"Why, I thought it would be obvious," I replied. "The China Sea!"

[I think it's important for me to note here that despite our informal studies and our choice and affirmation of religious observance as our way of life, we were still only at the beginning of our voyage and these three basic *mitzvos* were our anchors. If we could continue to observe these in China, we thought, the boat in which we were sailing would not founder. Too naive to know better, we were oblivious to the myriad difficulties Orthodox Jews encounter abroad.]

THE DATE OF OUR departure was now only a few days off and everything was set. The shipping company had collected our two small sea lockers, we'd finalized the arrangements for subletting our house, and I had picked up our airline tickets. Late one evening, Barbara turned to me with a serious expression on her face. "There's something I've been wanting to ask you," she said tentatively, "but I didn't know how to broach it."

"Well, just come out and say it."

"Okay. You've been wearing *tzitzis* now for about half a year. I really think you should start wearing a yarmulka all the time now, not just at home but outside the house too."

In a way I was glad Barbara had raised the subject because I'd been bothered by it for some time myself. I really had no objection to wearing a yarmulka when I went out, except that I thought I'd feel a bit strange and self-conscious. For four years all my colleagues, students and neighbors had seen me coming and going without one; to suddenly march into the office or the lecture hall with a strange-looking cap on my head would have made me feel very conspicuous. I told Barbara about my ambivalent feelings.

"And there's another thing," I went on. "You and I realize that we're just starting out in learning Torah. There are so many things we don't know or understand yet. Around here, hardly anyone wears a yarmulka. If people see you wearing one, they'll draw one of two conclusions: either that it's some type of affectation, some faddish conceit or pose, or that you're a rabbi. If they think you're a rabbi, they'll expect you to be knowledgeable about all sorts of Jewish questions. They'll expect some correlation between how you look and what you know, between how you appear and how you act. I really haven't been able to overcome my lack of confidence, you see. I'm still too unsure of myself."

"I really understand," Barbara said sympathetically. "Wait — I have an idea. In two days we're going to board an airplane to go halfway around the world. Why don't you start wearing a yarmulka the day we leave? In that way, you'll have a whole year to get used to it, and your colleagues and students and our neighbors will have a twelve-month interval between your appearance now and your new appearance when we return."

It was an ideal solution to my dilemma. On the morning of our flight, as I walked out the front door to the waiting taxi, I carried Dov Chaim in one hand, a suitcase in the other, and on my head was a knitted blue and white yarmulka. Later on, as we waited to board our flight to JFK, a man approached me. "Excuse me," he said, "are you a rabbi?"

WITH TWO SMALL children along, we decided to make several stopovers en route to Taiwan, thereby breaking up our long trip into more manageable stages. We visited friends in Tucson and San Diego, carrying our own food with us and supplementing it with fresh produce, and then spent three days at a Japanese guest house in Okinawa.

The guest house, a windswept aerie perched high above the beach, was nestled snugly against the mountainside, and the view was awe-inspiring. From the side of the structure, a row of spikey pines descended seaward, filling our room with fresh pine scent day and night. Surrounded by such scenic beauty and tended graciously by the kimono-clad daughter of the innkeeper, we savored our return to the Orient.

At the National Airport in Taiwan, Mei-Mei and her family (now enlarged by two for a total of six children) were waiting to greet us. It was a joyous homecoming. We all stayed overnight at a Taipei hotel, then journeyed once again to the fishing village of Tamsui and our two-bedroom cottage. It amused us to note that, while in the United States, Devorah had frequently been the focus of curiosity, here, Dov Chaim — who was blonde and fair-skinned — was the object of constant stares. The usually impassive Chinese who shared our train compartment were unable to restrain their heads from turning to get a better look at him.

When we arrived in Tamsui, we found that this time our Tamkang University hosts had provided us with a modern, well-equipped house. In fact, it looked like something that had been trucked in from Long Island and stood out in the faculty compound like an architectural displaced person or a guest who had overdressed for a party. It seemed our hosts had been a bit overzealous in their efforts to please us westerners.

Barbara made the organization of the kitchen the first order of business. She explained to Mei-Mei that, as Jews (*yoh-tai ren*), we had to obey certain rules and follow specific practices. She and Mei-Mei went shopping and purchased a new set of dinnerware, cookware, glasses and utensils. When they returned, she informed the by now bewildered Mei-Mei that it was necessary to take all the items to the sea. When Mei-Mei asked why, Barbara said simply that it was a requirement to immerse them in sea water.

After the briefest hesitation, Mei-Mei accepted this statement in her stride, as she did all things that life threw in her direction, and made arrangements for a taxi to drive us to a nearby inlet which flowed out to the China Sea. The taxi driver parked on the beach and we unloaded our assorted dishes and cooking implements, carried them several meters out into the water, and proceeded to immerse them one by one, while the driver looked on in disbelief. He turned to Mei-Mei and asked her why we were performing this peculiar ritual.

Mei-Mei, resourceful as ever, now considered herself an expert on interpreting Jewish customs to uninformed Chinese. "Oh, they are *yoh-tai ren*," she told him matter-of-factly. "There is old Jewish saying — 'The pot that knows the ocean will cook the fish, the dish that tastes the sea will serve it'."

WE WERE GENUINELY pleased that Mei-Mei was coping so well with our new lifestyle but I was sure natural human curiosity would eventually overcome native inscrutability. It didn't take long. One morning I noticed her standing off to one side and looking at me strangely. "Are you all right, Mei-Mei?" I inquired, giving her just the opening she'd been waiting for.

"Nothing with me," she said, "but Hwa-Peng and Bai-Lan not the same. Bai-Lan wears veil on her head and Hwa-Peng, blue and white butterfly perches on his. Early in morning, you stand by window wrapped up like lonely white cloud and bind your arm with black reins of horses pulling plow." She shook her head in confusion. "But also there is more quiet in your hearts, your faces are like spring breeze. The paper and pen are the same, but writing has changed."

"You're right, Mei-Mei, we are not the same." I phrased my explanation carefully, in a way that she could easily grasp. "We have moved closer to our traditional ancestors and closer to our God."

Mei-Mei nodded knowingly. "I am that way. I also honor the spirits. There is old Chinese saying, 'Even if tree is ten thousand feet high, leaves will fall to the roots.' *Yoh-tai ren*, Chinese — not so different." She had no further questions after that, not once throughout the entire year, no matter what seemingly odd practices we engaged in.

I T DIDN'T TAKE LONG for us to become reintegrated into our Chinese surroundings, and even Devorah adjusted well. Each morning, in the company of two small friends who also lived in the compound, Devorah would walk two kilometers down a dirt track and over a wooden bridge to the local kindergarten. All the school-children wore distinctive yellow hats with their names embroidered on the brims. Devorah's said Hsin-Mei.

At the start of each school day, Barbara and I would stand in our doorway and watch the small girls skip down the winding path until they became three yellow dots on the side of the mountain. Four years earlier, we had engaged in this same early morning activity with wistful expressions on our faces. Now we smiled happily with the knowledge that one set of bobbing pigtails belonged to our very own daughter.

Naturally, we wanted very much to sustain our developing involvement with Jewish life and were therefore pleased to discover that, during our absence, a Taipei Jewish Center had been organized. When we learned that High Holiday services were scheduled to be conducted there, we made arrangements to sleep over at an inn close to the Center for the duration of *Yom Tov.*

The Center was housed in a converted residence in the northern part of the city. It was an odd setting for worship, but somehow in keeping with the diverse group that assembled there. A few yards down the street stood a Nationalist Chinese military barracks. The polished bayonet of the sentry shone red with reflected light from the ornate altar of a Taoist temple that stood opposite the army quarters. Adjacent to the Jewish Center was the Saudi Embassy, and high above all rose the green edges of Ya Ming Shan (Grass Mountain).

By this time [1977], the American military forces in Taiwan had dwindled to a token presence, and the Center had inherited many religious articles from them, including a *sefer Torah* that had belonged to the former Jewish army chapel. There was no rabbi, no cantor. The congregants were left to their own devices. The major burden for conducting the service fell to a young, burly Israeli named Nachum, one of the few participants with some formal yeshiva training.

About sixty-five people attended the Rosh Hashanah services. They were Jews of totally dissimilar backgrounds and commitments, engaged in unrelated pursuits: businessmen and students, teachers, journalists and tourists. Some were alone, some were accompanied by their families. In addition to the Israelis, there were people from the United States, Germany, Canada, Holland, South Africa, France, Greece, England, Australia, New Zealand and Iraq — Jews from foreign lands praying in a foreign land. Their cacophonous chatter swiftly dissolved into a symphony of reverence, the many disparate tongues united by the Hebrew liturgy.

A sprinkling of Oriental faces in the modest crowd belonged to the Chinese spouses and children of some of the foreigners. I suddenly had an odd discomforting sensation. As I looked across at the Occidental-Oriental groupings, I felt as if I were viewing them through some new lens. My initial reaction was that they were curious and strange. Then I realized with a start that I was peering into a mirror: this was how Hsin-Mei and I must appear to others. I had long stopped thinking of Devorah as Chinese; she was simply my daughter. I almost never pondered her origins or contemplated the circumstances of her birth. Now, with an unexpected insight, I understood that what to me felt so normal and natural would be a constant source of curiosity to others.

YOM KIPPUR WAS a far more subdued affair. The day was gray, the air quiet. Grass Mountain seemed more distant. That morning we had an opportunity to learn something about Nachum, our amateur *chazan*. He had a rather brusque manner which served him as protective armor for an inner core of vulnerability. He told us he was born on Yom Kippur, as was his youngest son; and when he had returned from the hospital on the day of his son's birth, he found a message telling him that his brother had been killed in action in the Yom Kippur War. His story touched us deeply and somehow made the *Kol Nidrei* services even more meaningful.

The following afternoon a former rabbi, an eloquent speaker, delivered a sermon. It was said that he had studied in a yeshiva in Hungary and had left a large congregation in Los Angeles to take up residence in Taiwan. I found his speech particularly moving. "The first step of *teshuvah*," he said, referring to the writings of Samson Raphael Hirsch, "is the most essential and the most difficult for us to make, for there is within each and every one of us a small defender who is ready at all times to deny outright that we have done wrong at all, or at least to make excuses to mitigate and to cloak our transgressions." His delivery was powerful and his words seemed to strike a responsive chord among many of the congregants.

Later that evening, as the services drew to a close, the congregation sat huddled together. With the sounding of the *shofar*, an emotional wave rippled through the small room. I rose slowly to join the others for the "break-the-fast" meal and as I was leaving, I looked back for a moment. The rabbi's arm was around Nachum's broad shoulders, and there were tears in Nachum's eyes.

THE RAPID APPROACH of Sukkos, so close on the heels of Yom Kippur, took us by surprise. We had not yet developed a routine for *sukkah*-building and now we were confronted with the realization that we had only a few days for our construction project. Fortunately, there was no shortage of materials since an abundant supply of bamboo poles was available, and I immediately began to erect the frame for the *sukkah*.

Each day as I worked on the structure, Chinese passersby would stop to watch, scratch their heads and move on. As the *sukkah* grew more complete, the number of onlookers increased. I constructed a roof of small bamboo branches and leaves, making sure that there was enough open space among them to see the stars at night. On *erev* Sukkos I moved the kitchen table and chairs outside and set them up in the bamboo shack. Devorah helped with the decorations and, like Jewish children the world over, had a great time tying fruit to the overhanging limbs.

About an hour before candlelighting and the onset of the festival, Mei-Mei informed us that we had a visitor. A very serious looking university official was waiting at the front door. After exchanging courtesies, the official stated that he had been sent by the Dean of Studies who wished to know what aspects of our assigned accommodations displeased us.

The university would do everything in its power, he said, to oblige us.

We stared at the official in confusion. Several times we had expressed our gratitude to our hosts for the truly delightful accommodations. How could they possibly have gotten the impression that we were dissatisfied? We assured our visitor that the cottage was ideal and that we were very pleased and appreciative.

Now it was the official's turn to look perplexed. "If that is the case," he stammered, "why are you moving out of this house and building a new one outside?"

Mei-Mei, as usual, was listening from the wings. Before we could reply, she inserted herself into the conversation and calmly explained, "Tomorrow is fifteenth day of eighth lunar month. Chinese celebrate mid-autumn Moon Festival. Chinese eat mooncakes and walk in light of moon. Hsu Syen-Shung and Hsu Tai-Tai* are *yoh-tai ren.* They celebrate festival by eating and living outside, like old Chinese saying 'to wear moon on your head, and use stars as your cloak'."

"Oh, now I understand," the official said with a smile. "I did not realize that our customs were so similar! *Gung Hsi! Gung Hsi!*"**

"*Chag sameach!*" we replied.

* Mr. and Mrs. Hsu.
** Happy holiday.

EVERY SUNDAY MORNING Devorah attended Hebrew classes at the Jewish Center along with other Jewish children from the Taipei area. Their teacher was Mrs. Arieli, who came from Tel Aviv, and she taught the *alef beis*, Jewish history and religious customs. I would travel with Devorah and wait in the lounge until her class was over, passing the time in conversation with the other parents and visitors at the Center.

One morning I met a charming elderly woman who told me she was a former resident of Tientsin which, along with Harbin and Shanghai, had once had a flourishing Jewish community. In one wrinkled hand the woman held a chased silver cigarette holder and in the other, a glass of strong tea. Smoke from her cigarette wafted around her fragile features as she sat draped over the wicker chair like a faded lace curtain in a Victorian parlor. When she spoke, her voice seemed to come from far away, from remote hills and distant forests.

"We were a well-to-do Russian family," she said as she sipped her tea, "and Papa of course supported all the Jewish organizations in Tientsin, but he sent his children to be educated in the classical Russian manner. I learned to speak Russian, French and English, but not Hebrew. Our social circle was international; our religion, Zionism. Still we kept kosher, and I knew the beauty of the festivals and grew up proud of my Jewishness. We continued to lead a full and active communal life, even after Papa's death." The woman gazed nostalgically at the stand of bamboo waving in the yard and for a moment I feared she would not continue. She needed no encouragement, however, and in fact seemed pleased to have an audience for her reminiscences.

"All this changed quickly with the Revolution," she continued. "I was preparing to leave China with my mother in 1949, but the day before our departure, I realized it was Papa's *yahrtzeit*. The Communists had not yet totally curtailed our movements, so I went the next morning to the synagogue.

"When I arrived, I saw two Chinese men by the door. One was the caretaker who greeted me; the other, a stranger I did not know. The sexton allowed me to enter the synagogue. It was quiet and the morning light was soft and warmed the room. I stood next to the seat which my father had always occupied, a seat near the *bimah* in recognition of his prominence in the community. I recited the prayers I had learned as a child. As I finished, I looked up and saw the Chinese man I did not recognize. He was wrapped in a *tallis*, praying, a figure of great dignity. He prayed with intensity and strength. Our eyes momentarily met, and then I left him, praying alone. The next day we embarked on our journey to Israel." Again she paused as she relived these moments in her mind.

"A number of years later, I was in the Galilee visiting close friends who had also emigrated from China. They lived on a *moshav* and had adapted well to life in Israel. They had somehow managed to bring with them many things from China, whereas we had not. It was wonderful to hold these precious, familiar items in my hands again.

"That evening we discussed an article that had been written recently by [then Israeli president] Yitzhak ben Zvi. Ben Zvi, as you may know, was fascinated by the old Chinese Jewish community of Kaifeng. This community, which was founded by mideastern traders who had come along the Silk Road and remained, gradually became more and more Chinese until, with nearly total assimilation, it ceased to exist. Ben Zvi maintained that periodically a descendant of that community would emerge showing distinctive Jewish features, a Semitic nose or other typical trait. As one might imagine, this article was of great interest to us former residents of China.

"My gaze fell on a small figurine which my Galilee friends had perched on a corner table. It was a statue of an adult in Chinese attire, bent over, intent on the book he held. What arrested my attention were his features. His nose was larger than that of most Chinese and there was something familiar in his expression. 'Etta,' I said, 'this figurine must be modeled after one of the Kaifeng Jews. Look at his face!'

" 'Rena,' she said, 'you're crazy. You are still caught up with your experience in the synagogue. You see Chinese Jews everywhere!'

"That night in the guest room, I opened the window near my bed. You really feel Israel out here, I thought. The air was sweet, the moon filled the room with the same light I remembered from that morning in the synagogue. I went into the living room and brought the figurine back with me. 'Now, my friend,' I said to the little statue, 'you are really in Israel. Here, stand by the window, taste the air of our people.' Then I fell asleep.

"I woke the next morning to discover the figurine gone from the ledge. I searched on both sides of the window. I feared it had fallen and smashed, but there were no fragments anywhere. I felt so bad. My friends said not to worry and helped me search, but we could not find a trace. Etta said some passing schoolchild must have spied it and snatched it while I slept. I nodded and thought, 'And now my friend, you are somewhere in the Galilee, home at last, home in *Eretz Yisrael.*'"

A moment later, Devorah came dancing out of Hebrew class and launched herself into my open arms.

ONE DAY a notice arrived in the mail announcing that a visiting U.S. Army chaplain would be conducting the Friday evening services at the Jewish Center. We arranged to sleep over at the inn again so that we could attend, and we were really looking forward to a genuine Shabbos experience.

About twenty persons appeared at the Center on Friday night, most of them regular congregants. We learned that the chaplain was a Reform rabbi stationed in Korea, and that periodically he traveled to other areas in the Far East. He was introduced to the congregation by the president of the Center as Rabbi Abrams.

Rabbi Abrams expressed his pleasure at being able to join with the Taipei Jewish community in celebrating the Sabbath. He then went on to say that he had an admission to make: "I have a terrible singing voice." This statement was accompanied by a practiced smile. "I have therefore recorded all the Sabbath songs on tape. I will recite the appropriate prayers and at the point in the service which calls for a song, I will play the tape and you will have the benefit of listening to the beautiful voice of a noted cantor."

We couldn't believe he was serious, but after watching him use the recorder several times, we knew he was. It was difficult to decide whether this routine was more or less ridiculous than singing "Blowin' in the Wind" on Rosh Hashanah.

At the conclusion of the service, I approached the rabbi. "Rabbi Abrams," I said, "may I make a suggestion?"

"Certainly," he replied affably.

"Next time you visit, I will bring a tape recording with the appropriate congregational responses. Your tape will provide the leader's portion, and my tape, the congregation's. Your tape will lead and mine will follow. At the beginning of the service we will both place our recorders on the *bimah* and start them, and then you and I can go out for a drink."

Having said this, I wished the rabbi a "Good Shabbos" and rejoined Barbara who was waiting outside.

AFTER THAT FARCICAL experience, we decided to spend our remaining *Shabbosim* in Tamsui. Each week Barbara would make home-baked *challos* and Mei-Mei would prepare a special fish. When we first arrived in Taiwan, we didn't know what we would use for *kiddush* since there was no kosher wine to be had on the entire island, so out of necessity, we began to prepare our own homemade product. We obtained a very large earthen jug and purchased from the outdoor market several gallons of raisins and currants. For each gallon of raisins and currants, we used one gallon of boiling water and a variety of spices, such as cloves and ginger. We allowed the liquid to stand in a cool room for three days and then strained the mixture. Adding three pounds of lump sugar per gallon, we stirred until all the sugar dissolved. We poured the entire concoction into the earthen jar and placed it in a cool, dark place to ferment. When the fermentation process ceased, we strained the liquid once more and bottled the wine. This operation provided us with a supply which sufficed for the whole year.

Another problem we encountered concerned Shabbos candles. While there was a ready store of white candles easily accessible, what we had not considered was the fact that in China white candles are associated with funerals and mourning. Mei-Mei became very agitated the first Friday night that Barbara lit white candles. "Bai-Lan, Bai-Lan, what you are doing? Do you not know it is bad luck to light white candles? People will think ghosts are in this house!"

From her reaction we understood that others would feel equally uneasy about our white candles and this would adversely affect the cheerful Shabbos atmosphere we were trying to create. We therefore substituted red candles for the white, as these are associated with happiness and good fortune.

Every *erev* Shabbos before sunset, I made it a custom to stroll with Devorah to a field beyond our house. There we waited while the wildflowers trembled in the late afternoon breeze, and watched the sea rise and fall below us and the changing color of the sun as it moved in the water. On the far bank, the evening mist haloed the snow white sails of the fishing boats. The pale moon, high in the clouds, stood patiently awaiting its turn to shine.

Like Rabbi Chanina and Rabbi Yanai, we welcomed the Sabbath Queen. In her company, we returned to our Shabbos table upon which lay two fragrant, glazed *challos*, a flask of heady raisin wine, and our glowing red candles.

IN MARCH, I received an invitation to deliver lectures in Korea, Hong Kong and Thailand, an opportunity that meant a great deal to me professionally. After carefully working out my schedule, I contacted each of the airlines I would be traveling on to make certain that they would be able to provide kosher meals on my flights. Each airline assured me that there would be no difficulty whatsoever.

At the outset of my trip, I boarded an afternoon China Airlines flight to Hong Kong. Shortly after takeoff, the food service began, and the stewardess presented me with a double foil-wrapped container, the printed label of which indicated that the contents were under the supervision of the Chief Rabbinate of Switzerland. I removed the protective foil and was delighted to find a main course of flanken and farfel in a gravy sauce.

Until that moment I had been unaware of the intensity of my craving for home-style dishes. I'm actually a less strict vegetarian than Barbara, and in the United States I often enjoyed the chicken portion served to us as Shabbos guests in the homes of nonvegetarian friends. Here, Mei-Mei did most of the cooking for us and, although she was a superb cook, her repertoire of Jewish-cuisine dishes was decidedly limited. Even if we had been able to acquire kosher meat, I doubt that stir-fried flanken could in any way resemble the succulent boiled-for-hours slab of meat that now lay steaming in my disposable container. I devoured this savory meal with gusto.

At the completion of my visit to Hong Kong, where my lecture was well-received, I boarded a morning Korean Airlines flight to Seoul. At breakfast time, the stewardess again produced a kosher meal, protectively shielded in foil, and my mouth watered at the prospect of digging into another new treat. I was only mildly disappointed to discover that the package contained...flanken and farfel. Not particularly appetizing at eight A.M., but still tasty and reminiscent of home, if I disregarded the hour.

The lecture series in Korea was very successful, but I didn't wait for kudos. I hurried to catch my Thai Airlines flight to Bangkok. The stewardess, elegantly attired in traditional Thai costume, graciously served the shiny silver package on an intricately carved, sandalwood tray. My suspicions were confirmed when I read the label affixed to the foil — "Kosher Meal: Flanken and Farfel in Gravy Sauce".

Twice more on the lengthy flight the Thai stewardess presented me with the identical, by now monotonous, meal. On the return Japan Airlines flight to Taipei, I already knew what to expect. Only intense hunger enabled me to pick my way through the seemingly endless portions of flanken and farfel.

When at last I returned home to Tamsui, I had an excited and happy reunion with Barbara, Devorah and Dov Chaim. Mei-Mei called cheerfully from the kitchen, "Hwa-Peng, I have welcome-home surprise for you. Bai-Lan tell me how to make *yoh-tai* food and I prepare special treat — farfel suey!"

THE HISTORY of Jewish settlement in the interior of China extended over a period of more than one thousand years and only came to an end in this century. A major factor in its demise was the drastic decline in Jewish knowledge. From the seventeenth century on, there was no rabbi in the community and eventually, no teachers and no awareness of Jewish traditions. In the mid-nineteenth century, a visitor wrote of the remaining 200 to 300 Jews: "They have lost their religion and are indistinguishable from the heathen. They have idols in their homes and no longer circumcise. In features, dress, habit and religion, they are essentially Chinese." In 1941, the Japanese then occupying the city issued a report stating that the Kaifeng Jewish population numbered 180 souls.

One of the last known Chinese Jews was discovered two years before our arrival by Rabbi Marvin Tokayer. While he was serving as spiritual leader of the Tokyo Jewish community, Rabbi Tokayer heard rumors about the man's existence. The subject fascinated him, but the only clue he had to the man's identity was a name — Shih Hung-Mo. Rabbi Tokayer flew to Taiwan to investigate, and found there were many people who bore the exact same name. He turned to the son of Chiang Kai-Shek for assistance.

Since every male had to serve in the military, and since

the names of all military personnel, past and present, are locked into Taiwan's modern computer, the correct Shih Hung-Mo was quickly located by simply sifting through a list of all individuals with that surname who listed Hebrew as a second language. Only one name emerged.

Like Rabbi Tokayer, we too could not pass up the opportunity to meet a member of this lost society of Jews and we began an investigation of our own. The president of the Taipei Jewish Community Center gave us Shih Hung-Mo's address but added a proviso. He said that while Mr. Shih acknowledged openly that he is Jewish, he preferred to keep his Jewish life private and was understandably selective concerning his visitors.

Barbara wrote to Mr. Shih in Chinese saying that, as it was only a few days until Passover, she and her family would welcome the opportunity to bring him Passover foods and *matzos*. Mr. Shih replied immediately and set a time for a visit.

Model in Beth Hatefutsoth of synagogue in Kaifeng, China.

AS WE WALKED DOWN the narrow lane en route to our appointment, we were struck by the tremendous coincidence of it all. Five years earlier, we had lived just a few minutes from this very spot. In fact, as we walked further, we could even see the outline of our old compound tucked behind the corner of a rice paddy. This brought a flood of memories. It was to this home that we had first brought our infant daughter, a tiny dark-eyed bundle acquired with no advance notice or preparation, a tiny Chinese daughter who had been the catalyst that altered the direction of our lives. And now, five years later, just a stone's throw from our former residence, we were on our way to keep an appointment with another Chinese Jew!

Mr. Shih was waiting outside to greet us. In appearance, he was indistinguishable from other Chinese, except that his eyes were rounder and the cast of his features heavier. We exchanged greetings, and he took us to his quarters inside a compound designated for retired military personnel.

Mr. Shih's cottage was a simple one-room affair and his narrow bedroom, which also served as a study, was filled with books, charts and papers. In the course of our visit, we learned quite a bit about our host's background.

Shih Hung-Mo, a bachelor in his fifties, had fled the mainland in 1949 along with many other Nationalist troops. His parents had still been alive at the time, but he was certain that by now they were dead. He had had two brothers, one who was killed in Mainland China by the Japanese, and one who was killed in Korea by U.N. troops. His grandfather had been an herb doctor, and his father, an itinerant merchant.

As a young man, Mr. Shih had traveled with his father through the Middle East to Persia and as far as Haifa. He recalled his father pointing out gravestones with Hebrew inscriptions in a cemetery there. Once, during a visit to Shanghai, he showed a genealogy which had belonged to his grandfather to a rabbi from Minsk. The rabbi examined the document and said Mr. Shih's ancestors had indeed been

Jews. Encouraged by this rabbi to study Hebrew, he taught himself to read and write the language. He was very proud of the examples of his written work which he showed us.

While he was growing up, Mr. Shih's family celebrated three Jewish holidays — Rosh Hashanah, Purim and Passover, along with three Chinese holidays — New Year, Moon Festival and Dragon Boat Festival. He never ate pork products, he said, because he had been told by his grandfather that "we do not eat pork." Once, when he was visiting Kaifeng, he found only three Jewish families, all of whom had been reduced to poverty and who scratched out an existence as hawkers and pedicab drivers. They knew they were descendants of Jews, but knew nothing of Judaism.

Mr. Shih took a special liking to Devorah. He seemed genuinely pleased that she had been converted to Judaism, perhaps because he saw her as a link in a chain reaching back over thousands of years. He knew that assimilation, intermarriage and the open receptivity of Chinese society had, with the exception of himself, erased his entire community. Through Devorah and others like her, the existence of Chinese Jews might yet continue.

After an hour or so of such pleasantries, we gave Mr. Shih the Pesach food and *matzos* and wished him goodbye. He walked with us to the lane, where we took our leave. We had gone just a few steps when he called, "*Le-shanah haba'ah be-Yerushalayim* — Next year in Jerusalem!"

FROM TIME TO TIME I visited and lectured at various colleges and universities other than the ones where I was teaching, but after my flanken-and-farfel fling, I stayed closer to home base. On one such occasion I traveled to Kaoschung in southern Taiwan by rail, an experience I always found enjoyable.

The first-class compartments were quite comfortable. Blue-uniformed attendants served tea and provided warm compresses throughout the journey for the passengers to use to refresh themselves. Outside the window, the scenes were kaleidoscopic. Rice fields, barren after the harvest, lay sad and dispirited across the landscape. Around a sharp bend, a fragile suspension bridge suddenly appeared and below its delicate canopy, children waded in a creek. Slow-moving water buffalo regarded the passing train with tolerant indifference.

On this particular trip, the train made a number of stops en route to discharge and pick up passengers, and at Tainan a woman boarded carrying a very large clay jar. She sat down next to me and tried unsuccessfully to wedge the jar into the area between the seat in front of her and her own. Since this space was far too small to accommodate the vessel, she had to awkwardly balance the greater portion of it on her knees and lap. I had never seen anyone bring such a large, bulky item into the passenger compartment.

Prompted by the partial intrusion of the jar into my own space, I asked the woman why she did not simply put the item in the baggage compartment. "Oh, no!" she exclaimed. "That is impossible." The train sped on through mountain passes and terraced fields. After an interval of about fifteen minutes, my curiosity overwhelmed me.

"I'm sure this container is very heavy and must be quite uncomfortable for you to hold that way. Why do you say it would be impossible to store it with the baggage?"

"Why, it would not be respectful!"

This response confused me even more. "I don't understand," I said. "How could checking this item into the baggage car be disrespectful? There are no people traveling in the baggage car. It couldn't possibly disturb anyone there." I placed extra emphasis on the last word as I shifted again in my seat to prevent the rough edges of the receptacle from snagging my pants leg.

"Oh, I could never let this out of my sight," the woman said with conviction. "It would not be filial!"

"Filial?" I repeated, now totally puzzled. "What do you have in that urn?"

"My father," she declared.

"Wow!" I thought, suddenly remembering the extraordinary lengths to which Chinese went in fulfilling their obligations to parents. "Good thing I'm not a *Kohain*!"

Chapter 10

WHILE BARBARA and I struggled with Chinese customs and mores, little Devorah was waging a battle of her own: to conquer Chinese calligraphy. Written Chinese, unlike the writing of most other languages, is not composed of an alphabet. Each Chinese character or ideogram stands alone, representing an isolated picture or meaning. There are thousands of separate characters, formed by horizontal and vertical lines, dots, hooks, and slanting strokes, and learning to recognize and write them all is a slow and arduous process.

Most people find it quite difficult to grasp the technique of stroke-making, so it's best to begin training at an early age. Starting with kindergarten, Chinese children begin learning to make very simple lines and at least one hour a day is devoted to practice. Devorah, along with her classmates, faced the demanding task of learning how to write by copying Chinese characters over and over again.

To the Chinese, calligraphy is not mere handwriting; it is as much an art as painting is. In order to be considered calligraphy, writing must show originality, style, strength and personality. The modern Chinese philosopher Lin Yutang wrote that, "Every horizontal line is like a mass of clouds in battle formation, every hook like a bent bow of great strength, every dot like a falling rock from a high peak, every turning of the stroke like a brass hook, every drawn-out line like a dry vine of great age, and every swift and free stroke like a runner on his start." To this day, Barbara and I believe we can detect the influence of Chinese calligraphy on Devorah's written Hebrew and English.

Calligraphy is both the most esteemed and most popular Chinese art form. From childhood, affection and reverence for the written word is instilled in the Chinese heart and in every home one finds at least a few pieces of calligraphic work. Schoolchildren are taught never to tear up a sheet of writing nor to misuse any paper with writing on it, even if it is of no further practical use.

On my first visit to China, I saw old men with baskets of plaited bamboo on their backs gathering up wastepaper from the streets and roads and I naturally assumed they were engaged in litter control. From time to time I observed them burning the collected paper in a little pagoda at the edge of the village. Later, I understood that the Chinese respect for written characters was so great that they couldn't bear to see them trampled underfoot or discarded in some disagreeable place. The little pagodas were called *Hsi-Tzu-Tu* — Pagodas of Sympathy and Compassion for Letters.

Speech and writing are two expressions of the same impulse — the need to convey our feelings, ideas, reactions and thoughts. One form operates through hearing, the other through sight; the one by sound from mouth to ear, the other by image from hand to eye. The Chinese have taken these two modes of communication and transformed them into exquisite aesthetic forms, clear and well-spoken. Spoken Chinese takes on the quality of music, and through calligraphy, written words reveal striking artistic images.

Just as there was something intrinsic to the Chinese language that inspired and elevated, so too, I discovered, with Hebrew. But while Hebrew writing also has a tradition of impressive decorative qualities developed by *sofrim* (scribes) over the ages, and spoken Hebrew has many aesthetic elements, it is not these aspects that evoke reverence. With diligent study of traditional texts and observation of learned individuals, Barbara and I eventually realized that the genius of the Hebrew language lies in its unique ability to serve as a vehicle for conveying *kedushah*, holiness and sanctity. While the ability to speak properly and render admirably written characters is the sign of a cultured Chinese, the ability to use language to extol God's virtues and acknowledge our indebtedness to Him is one of the signs of a good Jew.

Chapter 11

URING OUR first visit to Taiwan, Barbara and I reacted to the numerous temples, shrines, and altars conspicuous throughout the island as objects of curiosity and architectural, historical and cultural interest. These structures varied from tiny pagodas erected by farmers in their fields, to impressive temple complexes occupying large tracts of land and dominating mountain summits. We found the Chinese theological system to be a complex mixture of: pantheism, revolving around the forces of nature; cultism, focusing on individuals who, by virtue of their past deeds, had become deified and the objects of worship (it was often impossible to determine the point where historical fact evolved into myth); Buddhism, with its other-worldly devotion to Nirvana; Confucianism, stressing moral and ethical virtues based on the teachings of Confucius and his followers; and Taoism, with its principles of natural simplicity and humility as markers to the right way.

The average Chinese is not concerned with doctrinal distinctions; he draws on all these sources to fashion his own eclectic creed. It was particularly difficult for us to differentiate among the various deities and gods that populated a given temple. In a typical temple one might find ten to twenty sacred images, figures and relics coexisting, jointly governing the spiritual realms of their worshipers.

Often, however, a temple would be closely associated with a particular god and once a year a special day was set aside for honoring it. The figure representing the god or goddess would be removed from its customary place within the confines of the temple and paraded throughout the entire village or neighborhood precinct. These were colorful, dramatic events, and they attracted us along with all the villagers.

The noise of the pageants was always deafening. Strings of firecrackers several feet in length would erupt incessantly, with gongs, drums and bells adding to the din. The air would become thick with burning incense and the acrid smoke of spent fireworks until a smoky haze hung over the entire area. A number of devoted followers would fall into a hypnotic trance and engage in extraordinary acts such as walking on hot coals or lacerating their bodies with sharp instruments.

On our present visit, Barbara and I found ourselves growing increasingly uneasy around these displays and we consciously avoided any contact with the temples and their attendant rites. The one exception was the ancestorial shrines for the veneration and placation of the spirits of the dead by their living descendants.

On one of our Shabbos walks into the countryside, we struck out on a dirt path. We walked past rural farmhouses and cultivated fields set apart by dense stands of bamboo. In the distance we saw a large structure with the characteristic pagoda-like curved roof associated with temples.

Upon reaching the site, we were surprised to see that instead of the usual array of idols and figures, the structure contained an altar on which rested a number of wooden tablets. While inspecting the interior we were approached by a young man. We exchanged greetings and I asked him about the nature and purpose of the tablets and the building which housed them.

The young man explained that the wooden tablets

represented his family ancestors, both recent and remote. The inscriptions on the tablets recounted the character and deeds of the deceased and the building was his family's ancestorial hall. On certain occasions, an individual, acting privately or as representative of the entire lineage, would present food, drink or other favored objects at the ancestorial shrine.

At first I believed that divination, witchcraft and magic were the central elements of the living family members' involvement with their departed relatives. Eventually, I understood that remembrance of ancestral spirits was primarily another manifestation of the central place of the family propounded in Confucian philosophy. Confucius taught that ancestors should be respected as they were in their lifetime. The respect and the offerings which symbolized this respect should be expressions of filial piety and not a bargain for a blessing. Ancestral rites were to be performed not for any magical effect but as an expression of one's feeling for, remembrance of, and obligation to one's ancestors.

Yet, it was clear to me that there was another dimension to ancestor veneration. The relationship between ancestors and descendants was clearly reciprocal. The Chinese believed that the fortunes of the living could be improved by the efforts of ancestors, and the spiritual welfare of ancestors enhanced by the worthy actions of living descendants.

My introduction to this facet of Chinese culture coincided with the approaching *yahrtzeit* of my father. Barbara and I continued to broaden our understanding and appreciation of Judaism through independent study, and had brought a number of appropriate books with us to Taiwan, one of which was *The Jewish Way in Death and Mourning* by Maurice Lamm. In it I read that, "*Kaddish* is a spiritual handclasp between the generations, one that connects two lifelines."

While intellectually I recognized the uniqueness of Judaism, I couldn't help occasionally comparing Jewish patterns with certain features of the surrounding culture. Lamm's image of the handclasp seemed to capture the basic intent of the Chinese practice of ancestor veneration. The concept of a mutual and reciprocal relationship between the deceased and their descendants is also present in Jewish life: "the merit of the fathers Avraham, Yitzchak and Yaakov" is a central theme; we request of God consideration and mercy in recognition of their righteousness. At the same time, the deeds of the descendants can affect the parent even after the parent's death, through the merit of his or her children.

AS THE TIME FOR our departure from Taiwan drew nearer, Barbara and I wrestled with a number of confused and ambivalent feelings. On the one hand we felt a deep and genuine affection for the Chinese and Taiwanese people and an appreciation for their ancient traditions. On the other hand there were a number of practices and customs which not only differed from those of Judaism but were in direct opposition to Torah precepts. Foremost was the ritual life of the Chinese majority: their temples and the gods and goddesses, spirits and deities they housed were the essence of *avodah zarah* — idol worship.

Throughout the last month of our stay, Barbara and I were made guests of honor at a series of farewell parties and banquets. We purchased gifts for friends and relatives, packed our belongings and arranged for the shipping of our personal effects. After submitting final grades to the various departments where I'd been lecturing, I paid courtesy calls to a number of university and government officials to thank them for their kindness during my visit.

With these chores and obligations fulfilled, a vague, indefinable sadness overcame us. Early on our last full day, Barbara, Devorah and I set out on the same dirt path which we had followed on many of our Shabbos walks. The air was fresh and alive. The rising sun tamed the mountain chill. We walked in silence past familiar landmarks — an isolated farmhouse with its clutter of chickens and tools; a narrow brook in endless conversation with a neighboring willow;

the ancestorial shrine, its curved roof a red hand open to the sky.

This day we walked farther than usual, up a winding narrow path we had never taken. The bamboo closed in around us. Devorah grew tired and I carried her in my arms. We inched slowly through the moving yellow passageway, emerging some minutes later on the crest of a hill. In the shade of a tree we rested and ate the small meal Mei-Mei had prepared. The winding road we had traveled stretched out below us, and in the distance we could make out the sea.

That night, our last in Taiwan, Mei-Mei came to visit. She carried a small package wrapped in red cloth. "Bai-Lan and Hwa-Peng," she said in a soft voice, "we are one family. To the four seas, to the earth's distant corners, we stand as brothers, we stand as friends. Please accept small gift. It is our household god, Tu-Di-Geng — god of earth and all that is good in it."

Late that night when all was still and dark, I arose softly. I dressed quietly and went into the next room. I took Mei-Mei's gift, placed it into its cloth bag and walked down the winding path to the silent, overcast harbor. The fishing boats rose and fell in their sleep.

I placed the cloth sack on the ground. Glancing around, I found a large stone among the pebbles on the beach and hefted it in my hand. The words of *Hallel* reverberated in my mind: "Their idols are silver and gold, products of human hands. A mouth have they but they cannot speak; eyes have they but they cannot see. Ears have they but they cannot hear; a nose have they but they cannot smell. Their hands cannot feel, their feet cannot walk; they cannot utter with their throat.... The heaven is the heaven of *Hashem*, and the earth He gave to mankind." I struck the bag with the heavy stone, over and over again, until its contents were reduced to small bits and shards. Then I cast the bag into the sea.

The next morning, Barbara, Devorah, Dov Chaim and I left Taiwan.

PART FOUR:

daybreak

And [the stranger] said: "Let me go, for day is breaking!"

GENESIS 32:27

ARBARA AND I quickly fell back into all our previous routines after our return to the United States. As a result of our continually growing involvement with Judaism, however, we became much more active in the formal organizational life of the Jewish community. We joined the Orthodox synagogue and became members of the Jewish Community Center. I was elected to the board of education of the Hebrew Day School where Devorah was enrolled and became active in Federation and U.J.A. affairs. We were also participants in the Federation-sponsored Young Leadership group and I even had a regular column in the local Jewish newspaper. For the first time in our lives, certain broad social and political issues began to take on real significance: Israel and its role *vis-à-vis* world Jewry became a growing focus of interest.

It seemed odd that Israel had never before held any particular fascination for us. Barbara and I had traveled extensively, twice circumnavigating the globe, yet each time we had unconsciously avoided Israel. We had never discussed the matter openly; instead there was a sort of implicit understanding between us.

If I were to analyze our feelings at the time, I would say we were still very unsure of ourselves and our Jewish identity, and we feared that the physical reality of *Eretz Yisrael* would force us to confront questions we were not yet ready to face. But now, with each passing day, we felt ourselves becoming stronger in our commitment and more prepared to deal with these questions. We knew that when and if the opportunity to travel presented itself again, Israel was certain to be on the itinerary.

BY THIS TIME, I had been wearing a yarmulka for over a year, ever since we had left for Taiwan, and had lost all feelings of self-consciousness I had formerly experienced. It felt as natural to me as any other item of clothing. Abroad, I had had a number of amusing encounters because of it, once when I was visiting a development project in a remote section of rural Thailand. I had traveled first by bus, then ferry and jeep, and finally by foot. When I arrived, I entered the only general store in the region. The western proprietor took one look at me and my yarmulka and said, *"Vus macht ah Yid?"* which I gathered was the Yiddish equivalent of "How ya doin', buddy?"

I soon discovered that Jews are literally everywhere and it was not unusual at all to find them in what seemed the most unlikely places. My yarmulka was a point of reference for these "wandering Jews" whose religious identity seemed to revive during our encounters, no matter how brief. On another occasion, a group of Koreans approached me and, with broad smiles on their faces, pointed to my yarmulka and gave me a "thumbs-up" sign of approval. But there were also some less-pleasant events, such as the time when I unexpectedly found myself on a very slow-moving customs and passport control queue surrounded by a group of Libyan military personnel. Suddenly I felt very conspicuous in my yarmulka.

After a short time back in the United States, I realized a major difference between wearing a yarmulka in the Far East and wearing one in the local community where I now lived. Since I was working and residing in a setting where very few

Jews covered their head, I had unintentionally become a symbol of "the religious Jew". While previously I wouldn't have thought twice about going into a McDonald's with a colleague to "talk shop", I now understood that even if I didn't eat or drink a thing while inside, people would still wonder what "that religious Jew" was doing in McDonald's, or worse, mistakenly think I was eating there and that the place must therefore be kosher.

This pressure to set a "good example" did not exist at all in Taiwan where few people had ever heard of a Jew, and fewer still had any concept of appropriate Jewish behavior. I felt much more than before that I was on stage and that any unseemly or unbecoming behavior, even if unintentional, could reflect badly on all Jews.

I found that reactions to my yarmulka varied. Our gentile neighbors were, for the most part, quite accepting and even approving. Since the population of the city, and, for that matter, the entire state where we resided, tended to be conservative and traditional, there was an overall favorable attitude toward religion and religious observance. People in this area took their religion seriously, and every Sunday the church pews were packed. While not many of our gentile neighbors had any clear understanding of Judaism, the fact that we also took *our* religion seriously was something they could relate to and approve of.

The same was not always true of the other Jews living in the community. I detected a vague, amorphous antipathy towards me. I sensed these feelings most strongly when I was together with other Jewish faculty members, particularly those in the School of Social Work. It wasn't anything I could really put my finger on, or express in words, or even explain, yet when I joined a group at the university I noticed that the Jewish faculty among them seemed to tighten up and behave uneasily in my presence. I wasn't certain whether these feelings were real or imaginary, but the events of the next few months were certainly real.

Prior to my departure for Taiwan, the department faculty had voted not to renew the contract of a particular assistant professor. These decisions were always difficult, occasionally nasty, and an inevitable part of university life. During my leave, this former faculty member initiated a legal action alleging sex discrimination. He argued that the female applicant hired as his replacement was clearly less qualified than he was. He referred to the Affirmative Action guidelines used in hiring the female applicant and asserted in his brief that the decision not to renew his contract was based on extraneous, non-academic and non-professional criteria.

Although I had not been chairman of the department at the time that these events took place, I was serving as chair when the case came before the Federal District Court. Along with a number of other university officials, I was subpoenaed to testify before the presiding judge. The case had already received some national notoriety since it was thought that the judge's ruling could set a precedent affecting the limits of the Affirmative Action legislation.

The day before I was scheduled to appear in court, the defense lawyers from the U.S. Justice Department advised me that the presiding judge would not permit me to wear my yarmulka in the courtroom while giving testimony. The judge maintained that to make an exception in this case would open his court to a parade of costumes, many of which could be quite bizarre and disruptive to the decorum of the proceedings. The lawyers further advised that if I insisted on wearing my skullcap, I would be held in contempt of court and possibly even imprisoned.

Although I was aware that, strictly speaking, it was permissible for me to testify in court bareheaded, I felt that because such an issue had been made about my yarmulka, it was important that I stand firm. I told the lawyers that I had no intention of removing it. I then contacted the local director of the Anti-Defamation League. The director quickly mobilized his staff and arranged to post bail if the situation required it. At the last minute, a compromise was reached, and I was allowed to give testimony *in camera* (in the judge's chambers), with my yarmulka on.

AFTER THESE EVENTS, things quieted down and I assumed that would be the end of any controversy surrounding yarmulkas, but I was wrong. Several months later a graduate student came to my office, a young man in his mid-twenties, clean-shaven and neat, wearing a knitted blue yarmulka on his head. I knew him from our occasional meetings around campus and at Jewish functions, and I greeted him warmly. "It's nice to see you. What brings you to the sociology department?"

"I have a problem," he said, "and I was hoping you'd be able to help me with it. I'm finishing up my Master's degree in clinical psychology, and as part of my required course work, I have to do an internship in a setting where I can gain first-hand counseling and clinical experience. Another Jewish student, who's completing his M.S.W., and I both chose to do our internships with Jewish Family Services."

"That seems like a natural choice," I observed. "It's beneficial to all parties concerned. You gain practical experience dealing with clients from the Jewish community at large, and the agency gets two interns who are knowledgeable about Jewish life and committed to improving its quality."

"That's just the problem," the young man said. "You see, both the other student and I wear yarmulkas."

"I'm afraid I don't understand," I said, genuinely puzzled.

"Well, the director of Jewish Family Services says she won't let us begin our internships if we wear our yarmulkas, and now all the other approved internship slots are already filled."

"Wait a minute," I interjected, my voice rising slightly. "Let me see if I've got this right. You're telling me that the director of our local Jewish Family Service agency told you and this other student that you are *not* to wear your yarmulkas while you're serving as graduate interns?"

The student nodded his confirmation.

"Okay," I said, trying to remain calm. "Did she offer an explanation?"

"Yes. She said the yarmulka is a 'very salient symbol with significant emotive potential'. She said that for some clients the skullcap would 'evoke powerful feelings that might interfere with the therapeutic relationship' between the client and his or her counselor."

"And what do you think?" I asked.

"Well, I agree that the yarmulka is a symbol, but it is just one of many symbols which are connected to a person. My eyeglasses are a symbol, being male instead of female has symbolic meaning, my height and weight have symbolic meaning. If we try to control every symbol attached to us, a counselor would have to meet his clients while sitting behind a screen, and then he would still have to worry about the effect of his voice and the symbolic meaning of his words."

"And why did you come to see me?" I inquired, although I knew what his answer would be.

"Because you are the only faculty member on campus who wears a yarmulka, and because you're active in the Jewish community, and there was that business with you and the federal judge and your yarmulka, so I thought you might be able to do something...."

"All right," I said. "Thank you very much for letting me know about this. I'll see what I can do." After the student left, I phoned the director of the Anti-Defamation League. He was out of the office so I left word with his secretary for him to call me back as soon as possible.

That evening at home, I received his return call. "Henry, how are you? Thanks very much for calling back."

"No problem," Henry said amicably. "I'm sorry I

couldn't contact you before but I was out of town. How can I help you?"

"I really appreciated your prompt and effective assistance at the time I had to give testimony in court," I said, and went on to give a condensed report of my conversation with the psychology student. My instincts told me, however, to hold back some information.

"Well, Allan," he said when I completed my recitation, "that certainly sounds like a case of discrimination. I'd like to get moving on this right away. What's the name of the agency?"

"It's a local agency, right here in the city," I replied, still hedging.

"Yes, but if I'm to do anything, I'll need to know which one."

"Jewish Family Services."

There was silence on the other end of the line. Finally the director said, "Well, thank you very much. I'll look into it," and with that the conversation abruptly ended.

When I didn't hear from Henry for a number of days, I called his office but was unable to reach him and my calls were not returned. Finally, I decided to go there in person. The director greeted me and I asked what he'd been able to do about the situation.

"Well, it turned out that the two students have voluntarily agreed to remove their yarmulkas, so there was no need for our office to become involved."

I was incensed! "You know, Henry, there's something very wrong here. If this had been a Christian agency, like Catholic Charities or even some secular agency, you would have been down on them in a flash. I've seen how quickly your office can mobilize itself. But because in this case it was a Jewish agency that was acting in a discriminatory manner, you found it awkward and decided to do nothing. The whole business is two-faced. When *goyim* discriminate against Jews, it's a big thing, but when *Jews* discriminate against

Jews, it's better to look the other way."

"I think you're being unfair, Allan."

"You're entitled to your opinion and I'm entitled to mine!" I said indignantly, too angry to think of a more impressive parting shot. With these words, I turned on my heel and stalked out of the office.

I was still seething when I arrived home. "What hypocrites! Imagine, a Jewish organization forbidding the wearing of yarmulkas!"

Barbara exerted a calming influence. "Don't forget," she said, "not so long ago *you* didn't even wear a yarmulka. Now all of a sudden you're a big shot. If you keep this up I'm going to start calling you 'the Mad Hatter'. Look around you, Allan. People in this community have been trying hard for a long time to blend in with the majority, and most of them have succeeded very well. They've become excellent chameleons. The yarmulka is a visible sign that someone is a Jew. They don't *want* to appear different from anyone else! To them a yarmulka is something that shouts out, 'Look at me, I'm a Jew.' They can't handle it. You of all people should show more understanding."

"I hate to admit it," I said, "but you're right again." In fact I thought Barbara had put her finger on the reason my Jewish colleagues at the university felt uneasy and uptight about my head covering. "I'll just have to try not to let my yarmulka go to my head!"

YEARS LATER, Norman Goldwasser, a graduate student in psychology at my former university, wrote me the following letter:

> ...I have to tell you a wonderful story. While I was struggling on my thesis, I had to tackle the computer for data analysis, text processing, etc. It was very frustrating and difficult and the consultants usually didn't want to bother with an amateur like me. However, one young man went out of his way to assist me, sometimes even leaving the

consultant's office to help me in the computer room (which he wasn't supposed to do). Anyway, to make a long story short, we began to chat one day and I asked him what country he was from (he's Oriental). He told me that he was from Taiwan. So naturally I told him that I had a good friend who had lived in Taiwan and proceeded to describe you. He replied, "Oh, Dr. Schwartzbaum! He was my professor in Taiwan and he helped me to come to this university. In fact, when I saw your 'yamaha' I knew you must be a nice person like Dr. Schwartzbaum, and that's why I've helped you so much." You can't imagine what a profound effect that had on me. It just shows how far one's good deeds can spread. So, thank you for helping me complete my thesis!

If I'd needed any further confirmation of the righteousness of my position on the yarmulka issue, Norman provided it. But at the same time I knew that being right was not enough.

FINANCES DOMINATED the agendas of the Day School's board of education meetings. As a new member of the board, I soon realized that, with the school severely under-capitalized, educational programming and budgets were inextricably linked. The financial difficulties, I learned, were not a recent phenomenon; they began with the school's formation.

The Day School had originally been founded in response to the needs and through the efforts of a very small circle of parents affiliated with the Orthodox synagogue. Dissatisfied with the existing opportunities for Jewish education, a handful of congregants, together with their rabbi, opened an all-day Jewish primary school on the synagogue premises. With its student population numbering, on average, ten, the school might always have remained a very small enterprise identified with a minority segment of the Jewish community, except for one event of tremendous socio-political import — desegregation.

Confronted with court-ordered integration, Jewish parents in the city had, basically, three options. The first, to accept the new reality and adjust to it accordingly, meant in some cases enforced busing and a significantly altered school and classroom environment. A second choice was to relocate to the suburbs outside the city limits, where the percentage of non-white residents was very low. For many families who found it extremely difficult to sell their homes and move outside of the city, this option was not feasible. The third option was to enroll their children in a private, parochial school, of which there were two main types in existence: the newly emergent "Christian Academies" and the "old line" prep schools.

At the Christian Academies, however, the overt fundamentalism was so blatant and shrill that even the most assimilated Jewish families found it impossible to consider them suitable for their children. The prep schools, on the other hand, with their long tradition of serving the upper-class establishment of the state, provided a viable alternative for some. While these schools often had a religious association, it was viewed by most Jewish parents as rather innocuous and they deemed attending chapel a small price to pay for the considerable status enhancement. The main deterrent in this case was the exorbitant tuition, which was beyond the means of all but the wealthiest families. Many Jewish parents who would have sent their children to such schools simply could not afford to do so.

There remained a significant number of parents, therefore, who could not or would not accept any of the three options. Faced with this predicament, they began to enroll their children in the Jewish Day School. And as the school population began to expand, it soon became evident that the existing facility in the Orthodox synagogue was no longer adequate. A decision was made to build a new school, but because of the immediate demand for places, construction proceeded without the usual period of development and fundraising. Hence, from its inception, the school was faced with a sizeable mortgage debt.

The board of directors realized from the start that income from tuition would never cover operating expenses. A host of fundraising activities ranging from raffles to bingo was introduced, but the school continued to operate in the red.

The board decided to turn to the Jewish Federation for financial assistance.

A proposal was prepared and a meeting scheduled for its presentation. In the course of the discussion, one of the Federation representatives posed a question concerning the eligibility requirements for admissions. It was explained that the school was open to all Jews. The questioner then asked for the school's definition of "Jew". The principal, Rabbi Goldstein, replied that a Jew was anyone whose biological mother was Jewish or who was properly converted.

Still the questioner was not satisfied. "As you are well aware," he said, "our Federation is an organization that represents the entire Jewish community, not just one particular segment. We try to identify and meet the needs of all Jews, Orthodox, Conservative and Reform, as well as the unaffiliated. What would happen if two Jewish parents approached you wishing to register their child?"

"Why, I would be most happy to enroll their child," the principal replied.

"Now, what if the mother of the child was converted by a Conservative or Reform rabbi from our community?" the representative asked pointedly.

"Well, in that case, I would require that the child be properly converted before accepting him for admission."

"In other words, you do not accept the validity of a Reform or Conservative conversion."

"That is correct," Rabbi Goldstein confirmed.

"Do you realize," the Federation representative challenged, "that over ninety percent of the affiliated members of this community are members of either a Reform or Conservative synagogue? Furthermore, are you aware that the contributions of the ten percent of the community affiliated with the Orthodox synagogue constitute only two-point-one percent of the money collected in last year's campaign? You are asking this community to help finance a Jewish school which does not recognize its rabbis and considers many of its

Jewish members not to be Jews at all — the very same Jewish members who contribute significantly more money and time to the Jewish community than those individuals who refuse to acknowledge their Jewishness!"

The principal, obviously prepared for this argument, stated quietly, "Our school is indeed representative of the entire Jewish community. Our students represent a cross section of the various Jewish denominations. The issue you are raising pertains only to those cases where the mother of a potential student was not born a Jew."

"Indeed. But those individuals are also part of our community." The debate continued for another ten minutes before the chairman brought the meeting to an end.

Eventually, the Federation decided to provide some assistance to the school, assistance which, given the financial condition of the school, was critical to its continued survival. I realized that as soon as the school accepted such funds, it would lose some of its autonomy and would have to accommodate some of the interests of the larger Jewish community. This was inevitable, I felt, and to a great degree legitimate since the community at large, through the Federation, was helping to support the school's existence. I believed, however, that the policy of only admitting students who were halachically Jewish was inviolate.

The school board left the admissions decisions exclusively in the hands of the principal. The board believed that issues of a private nature such as adoption, conversion and remarriage which arose during interviews with parents of prospective students, were best handled confidentially by one person. I never questioned this policy until one day when I noticed that a certain child had been recently enrolled. I knew that in this case the mother had been converted by a Conservative rabbi in the community. I also knew that the family neither kept kosher nor observed the Sabbath. I couldn't make any sense of this, especially in the light of the requirements set forth for Devorah's conversion.

One afternoon after school, I dropped by the principal's office. "Rabbi Goldstein, do you have a moment?"

"Of course, Allan. Please come in and have a seat."

"Rabbi, something is troubling me," I said. "The new student who recently entered the third grade — how were we able to admit him? He isn't Jewish."

"What do you mean?" Rabbi Goldstein asked, taken aback.

"I happen to know his mother did not undergo a halachically valid conversion, and a child born to a non-Jewish mother, regardless of who the father is, has the status of a non-Jew. Her offspring, therefore, are obviously not Jewish."

"Yes, well, before we admitted him, the boy was converted with the approval of an Orthodox *beis din*. Since he was previously circumcised, the rite of *hatafas dam bris*, which involves a pinprick letting a spot of blood, was performed by a *mohel* and he was immersed in the *mikveh*."

"That's all very well and good," I said, "but his parents are not observant. The home is not a real Jewish home."

"Yes, I realize that is a problem, but we received a rabbinic ruling, a waiver of normal procedure, for this special situation from an esteemed *rosh yeshivah*."*

"Why? Is this child a special case?"

"No," Rabbi Goldstein said, "he isn't special in himself, but he represents a special situation."

"You mean that converting children in this way is now the policy of the school?"

"Yes," the rabbi answered.

"You mean that whenever non-Jews want to enroll in the school, you dunk them in the *mikveh* and — hocus-pocus — they're Jewish?"

---

* Varying positions on this subject have been taken by competent rabbinic authorities, dependent on considerations and conditions that obtained at other times and in other locales. The ruling related here applied to this time and this place.

"Now, wait a minute. You know that's not what I mean. First of all, the very fact that the parents want to enroll the child in the Day School says something about the possibility that the family may one day lead an observant life. Righteous Jews have been known to emerge from non-observant homes — look at your own family."

"I'm sorry, Rabbi, but I have to disagree. First, you are assuming that the motivation to send the child to this school is a desire to provide a stronger Jewish education. While one might hope that's true, it's just as likely that the motivation is the parents' desire not to bus their child to a school where he has to learn with a lot of non-whites. You yourself have seen that many parents who started out in the Day School transfer their kids to public schools after they move to the suburbs.

"Second, I know you're knocking yourself out to make this the best school possible. I know the kind of workday you put in, both inside and outside of school, but why kid ourselves? As long as the community and family context remain unchanged, this school is never going to transform its students into observant individuals, let alone their parents. Just look at the pressure we get from the Board of Education to cut back on Jewish studies in order to give the children more math, more science, more music, anything — as long as it's not more Jewish studies! Just last month you had to give in on the issue of compulsory wearing of *tzitzis*. In the beginning, it was required; now it's optional." The principal could not deny anything I said.

"Let me ask you, Rabbi," I went on, "how is it that when my wife and I wanted to convert our daughter, we were given this speech: 'Oh, it doesn't matter if the child is Chinese or Indian or Eskimo. What matters is if the home is observant.' The man who said that was absolutely correct. How can you make a child Jewish if immediately afterwards he enters a home where he can't live a Jewish life?"

"There are other considerations," the rabbi said evasively. "For example, there is the survival of the school and the overall benefit to the Jewish community. You were at the meeting with the Federation — you saw the way we were attacked. This policy allows us to accept the children from all segments of the community while holding the line on Orthodox conversions. By validating the conversion of minor children, even though the family is not observant, we may encourage some level of commitment, we may instill some level of Torah values."

"Now you're not telling me that what matters most is the survival of the school! Survival at what cost? To create Jews who will live like *goyim*? What you're saying is that it doesn't matter if the child is Indian, Eskimo or Hottentot, what matters is that the school — and your job — survive!" I immediately regretted that remark. Rabbi Goldstein was not only a rabbi and the school principal, he was also my friend. Furthermore, I knew better than most how vital the school's continued existence was.

LATER THAT EVENING, I went to speak to Rabbi Fried, who had been so instrumental in Devorah's conversion. He confirmed that he had likewise sat on Jewish courts converting children in this manner, although at first he had been reluctant to participate. The ruling from the recognized rabbinic authority made him decide to cooperate. "I know how you feel," he said. "This is a normal part of the *ba'al-teshuvah* experience. You feel betrayed. You made a sincere, serious commitment to a new way of life, and it's only natural for you to expect the individuals who introduced you to this way of life and encouraged you to make it your own to live up to the standards they demanded of you.

"Allan, you are a *farbrenter*, a true believer, and all true believers sooner or later get disillusioned and have to confront the real world. There are a lot of grey areas in life — not everything can be labeled black or white — and halachic rulings must be made in order to cover the greys. Rabbinic authorities rule on how *halachah* is to be applied to present situations. When the situation changes, so must the ruling.

"You have a right to be disappointed and angry, Allan, but you also have a responsibility to try and understand."

It was very difficult for me to do so. True, Barbara and I had been resentful when the first Orthodox rabbi we met refused to convert Devorah on the very grounds that were at issue here. But as Barbara had later indicated, we were not yet ready to make the necessary concessions. By the time Rabbi Fried had come into the picture, we had come a long way and were far more inclined to accept the conditions he stipulated. We were also far better off for having done so. Our lives and Devorah's were surely enriched by religious observance and we avoided all the conflicts that inevitably arise when a child is taught one thing in school and sees the opposite at home.

But Rabbi Fried and others felt there were more pressing considerations. "Let's examine this situation," he said. "We have an existing reality: the rate of intermarriage between Jews and gentiles is increasing at an alarming rate. As a result we face a major issue concerning the status of children born to gentile mothers who have not converted properly. Each year there are more and more such children. What will be their ultimate status? Are they to be forever excluded from the Jewish community, or can they be brought into the fold in some manner compatible with Jewish law? By converting them as minors in an Orthodox manner, we bring them halachically into the Jewish community. Now, since these conversions take place before the children are able to exercise their own reason, it follows that when the children reach the age of thirteen years and a day for boys, and twelve years and a day for girls, they should be informed of the conversion. Their Jewish status automatically obtains as long as they don't reject it."

"Fine," I said, "but what happens if these children reach the age of twelve and thirteen and a day, and they're still not observant? What happens if they still eat *treif* and continue to violate the Sabbath? Clearly they would seem to be lacking in *kabbalas mitzvos*, awareness of and commitment to observe Jewish commandments. Yet they have every reason to think of themselves as Jewish. They underwent an Orthodox conversion registered with the Rabbinical Council of America; they went to an Orthodox Day School. Why shouldn't they consider themselves Jewish? But are they Jewish? What if a Jewish boy married a girl converted in this way — are their children Jewish?"

Rabbi Fried stood up from his chair. He walked to his bookshelves and back again. "I don't know," he said quietly, "I really don't know."

THE CONTROVERSY over the Day School admissions policy was only the first of many in which I became involved as Judaism became an increasingly significant factor in our lives. The next arose when a group of Russian Jews arrived in the city. While Barbara and I were troubled by the broader question of "dropouts" who, after leaving the Soviet Union, in large numbers had chosen to bypass Israel in favor of the U.S., we actively joined the community effort to ease their resettlement.

On the Russians' first *erev Shabbos* in their new homes, Barbara organized several women to call on each new family and present them with flowers, Shabbos candles and candlesticks, and kosher wine. We also helped to collect clothing and furniture for those in need.

Shortly after their arrival, I learned that the Russian children were being enrolled in the local public schools. I was appalled.

"This is ridiculous!" I told Barbara. "They should be going to the Hebrew Day School." When I questioned the community leaders about the matter, I was told that the public schools would facilitate their integration into American society. In any event, they added, the Russians were entitled to exercise free choice. After all, weren't they living in a free country now? I demanded an opportunity to speak before the local committee charged with overseeing the resettlement effort.

At the next meeting, I expressed my views on the subject. "When these individuals lived in the Soviet Union," I said, "they made an unparalleled attempt at integrating with the Russian people and with Russian culture, and despite this they were pushed away. No matter how hard they may have tried to forget they were Jews, Soviet society reminded them. Their religion was stamped on their identity card, they were reminded of it when they applied to university or when they were overlooked for promotion. No matter how hard they tried to be good Soviet citizens, they were still discriminated against as Jews.

"Yet, unlike the refugees of previous generations, today's immigrants leave home with conflicting emotions — hope and confusion — and often the confusion is stronger than the hope. While in the Soviet Union they were made to feel like Jews in spite of being Russians, in the United States they still feel like Russians in spite of being Jews. They are discovering how really deep their ties are to their native language and culture, and don't even know how much they've distanced themselves from their faith. This situation demands sensitivity and understanding on our part. It is as important to make our new neighbors feel comfortable and secure with their Jewishness as it is to make them feel comfortable with being Americans. Eventually, they will become Americans regardless of our efforts. They may stop being Jews, however, without our encouragement and support."

In the end, two out of sixteen Russian children enrolled in the Day School. I chalked that up as a victory — a small one, perhaps, but a victory nonetheless.

ON ANOTHER OCCASION, the Suburban Board of Education announced that two school days lost due to heavy snows were to be made up by holding classes on two Saturdays. They justified this decision by claiming that, since the law required scheduling a specific number of school days per year, this compensation arrangement promised the least disruption. There was an immediate outcry from several local rabbis and various Jewish organizations. After a great commotion, the Board of Education revised its original decision and extended the school year by two days.

To me, the victory seemed a hollow one. I submitted an article for my column in the local Jewish newspaper ridiculing the self-congratulations that followed the Board's reversal. I wrote that the wrong question had been asked in the dispute. The issue was not, "Why should Jewish students be made to attend classes on their Sabbath?" but rather, "What would these Jewish students be doing if they *weren't* attending classes on their Sabbath?" Would they be praying in the synagogue? Would they be honoring the Sabbath by joining their parents at the Shabbos table? Would they be reflecting on God's dominion over the world He created? Very unlikely, I said. These students who had been saved from the hands of an unenlightened gentile Board of Education would be using their now-free Sabbath to see the latest film, to take a spin in the car, to party. The article embarrassed some in the Jewish community, but the majority simply ignored it.

EVEN RIDING a hobby horse can be wearing and my very time- and energy-consuming communal activities were beginning to exhaust me. I therefore looked upon our annual visit to my mother in Florida as a welcome respite.

My mother lived in a subsidized senior citizens' apartment house in Orlando, a twelve-story building which had been built with the financial and organizational support of the local Jewish community. The residents, while reasonably self-sufficient, had the assistance of a staff concerned with their safety and security. With its cast of local characters and personalities, its cliques, squabbles, kindnesses, and even an occasional romance, the building was a geriatric microcosm of a high-rise neighborhood. Barbara and I would seasonally enter this world, first by ourselves, then with Devorah, and later with Dov, and each time come away with new insights and good feelings.

As we became more involved with and knowledgeable of Judaism, I became aware of certain things I had never noticed before. I realized that the conception I had of all elderly Jewish people as being religious was incredibly naive. In my mind, I had somehow come to equate Jewish observance with that generation of men and women who were born in Europe and spoke Yiddish. Maybe it was all those calendars and paintings depicting old rabbis studying and praying, or perhaps because in the past, on the rare occasions that I had gone to synagogue, I encountered very few young people, that I had come to sincerely believe that religion was the domain of the elderly. Now I recognized that there was no necessary correlation between age and religiosity.

While almost all the residents in my mother's building were Jewish, very few were actually Orthodox. My mother was one of the exceptions. As Barbara and I gradually became more and more observant, my mother changed along with us until she slowly recovered the Jewish practices she had left behind in the Poland of her youth. She would shake her head with exasperation when she saw her co-residents using the washing machines on Saturday. "They have all week to do their wash," she would say. "It's not like they're working or have some place special to go on the rest of the days. Most of the time they're just sitting outside or watching their soap operas on TV. So why do they *davka* have to do their wash on Shabbos?"

Within the small world of the apartment building, private affairs often became public concerns. My mother tried to avoid the busybodies, but considering their numbers, this was often impossible. One afternoon she and I entered the lobby after a short walk and we sat down on a small sofa in the foyer. The two-seater could accommodate us sitting close together but comfortably. After a few moments, a stoutish lady planted herself down in the narrow remaining space on the couch. My mother looked at her and, with the smallest trace of irritation in her voice, said, "We are having a *private* conversation." The new arrival was not moved by this comment and remained seated. My mother shrugged her shoulders and we went on with our talk.

After about five minutes the woman looked up and announced, "You're right!" then hoisted herself up and vacated her seat.

On the elevator, in the lobby, outside on the patio, wherever they congregated, the residents always reacted warmly to the children. A delegation came up to Dovie who, because he was not yet three, had his uncut hair put up in a long ponytail, and said, "Hello, darling. What is your name?"

"Dov Chaim Schwartzbaum," he replied proudly.

At this point the questioners looked to Barbara and me for help. "But what is her *real* name?"

"That *is his* real name."

The dual realization that *she* was a *he* and that that *was* his *real* name led to even more confusion, and the clarifications went on for half the afternoon.

By this time Devorah had made quite a number of trips to visit Grandma and the residents had come to know her and look forward to her arrival. Her sparkling personality won her many friends and admirers and we observed her reaching out to and befriending some of the lonelier ones. All in all, it was a mutually beneficial and rewarding visit. Upon our return home, Devorah happily reported to all her classmates that she had just come back from visiting her "one hundred *bubbies* and *zaidies*."

Soon, however, this cheerful interlude was forgotten and we found ourselves once again in the thick of community affairs.

The Taiwan Jewish Center, where Devorah attended Hebrew classes, made a "birthday party" for Israel's 30th Independence Day.

Our gan-gya ("adopted family") — our closest friends in Taiwan.

On sabbatical in Israel, our first stop was the Kotel.

Our apartment in Maalot Dafna was cramped and run-down but the special light of Yerushalayim transformed it into a palace.

Dovie and Dahveed joined me for Shacharis.

For Dahveed and Shmuel, as for all of us, visiting Rochel's parents in Florida is a delight. We brought the bridal vanity table (background) back with us from Taiwan.

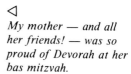

My mother — and all her friends! — was so proud of Devorah at her bas mitzvah.

The poster Devorah made reads "Welcome" in Hebrew and Chinese (note characters between the figures). ▽

One of Devorah's all-time favorite pastimes!

In HAGA, the Israel civil guard, I serve in a unit called "ZACH" — zihui challalim, which is responsible for the identification of bodies ר"ל so that they can receive a proper burial.

By Yehudah's bris I had learned the secret of successful delivery of divrei Torah —brevity! Rabbi Shalom Gold, who was sandak, is seated to my left.

174

Devorah's brothers are as enchanted with her as she is with them.

Our life is so different now that we all have trouble believing that those strangers in Devorah's baby album are really us.

The boys suggested a Chanukah sequel to this book called "The Bamboo Dreidel." Rochel, who is a fabulous cook, offered "The Bamboo Kneidel." Devorah's contribution, for which there was a general consensus, was "The Bamboo Meidel." I abstained.

Devorah's nursery school diploma; (top)   *"Hsin-Mei"'s kindergarten diploma. (bottom)*

מדינת ישראל

בית הדין הרבני האזורי
ירושלים

ב"ה, תאריך **ב' שבט תשמ"ו**
12.1.86
מספר **ו/2859**

המבקשת – שוארצבוים דבורה
הנדון – אשור גיור

פָּסַק דִין
================

אחרי שמוע דברי המבקשת והוריה מאשרים את הגירות של המבקשת
דבורה שורצבאום, נולדה כב' אייר תשל"ב (6.5.72), מס' זיהוי,
015478837, שסודר ע"י הרב אליהו מאיר דייויס פ בפלורידה
ארה"ב,

בית הדין הרבני האזורי ירושלים

נאם: _____

נאם: _____

נאם: _____

The Israeli Chief Rabbinate's confirmation of Devorah's conversion.

178

1 BECAME SO wrapped up with my skirmishes with the local Jewish establishment that I frequently lost my sense of proportion and even Devorah became an occasional victim of my overzealousness. Once, the Day School, in its continual quest for funds, organized a magazine sales project, with the students playing the role of sales force. The children were to sell subscriptions to their neighbors, friends and relatives, who could choose from a list of over seventy-five titles, and the school would realize a commission on all sales. Like her classmates, Devorah was anxious to do her share.

Recalling an episode from my youth, I cursorily examined the list on the afternoon Devorah brought it home to make certain that the students would not unwittingly be selling any explicit adult magazines. No such magazines were included, but I discovered something equally disturbing. Interspersed throughout the list were nearly a dozen Christian publications!

I immediately phoned the principal, Rabbi Morris Jacobson, who this year had replaced Rabbi Goldstein. "Rabbi," I declared, getting right to the point, "we will have to delete a number of items from the magazine list. It's wrong to involve children from an Orthodox Jewish Day School in the dissemination of Christian literature."

The principal, taken by surprise, was momentarily confused. "I'm not sure I follow you. What exactly are you referring to?"

I replied hotly, "For your information, Rabbi, on the list of magazines the children are selling there are a number of Christian publications. Let me read some of the titles to you." I proceeded to call off some of the more obvious ones. "Surely you agree that this is totally inappropriate."

The principal took his time responding. From the day of his arrival, Rabbi Jacobson had taken what I viewed as an untenable position *vis-à-vis* the local community. Increasing enrollment at any cost was his goal, and to this end he was prepared to sacrifice almost any principle or registration requirement. Not surprisingly, we frequently found ourselves at loggerheads over one issue or another. "Now, Dr. Schwartzbaum, I don't know why you should be so upset. These titles comprise only a small percentage of all the magazines on the list."

"Look here, Rabbi," I insisted, "I don't care if there's only *one* such magazine on the list! *One* is too many. What if there were a Jews-for-Jesus monthly included — how would you feel about our students hawking such a publication door to door?"

"But there is no such magazine on the list."

I thought he was being intentionally obtuse and this increased my fury. "Of course," I said impatiently, "but the difference between that fictitious title and the ones our students will be selling is only one of degree. It's simply not right!"

The principal tried a more conciliatory tone. "What do you propose?"

I suggested that, since we were already committed to the project, we cross off the lists all such publications before sending the children out canvassing for sales. The principal disagreed. "Imagine what our gentile neighbors would think if someone presented them with a list on which all the Christian magazines were crossed off," he said. "How would *you* react if someone came to your home with a list on which all the Jewish publications were crossed out?"

"In that case," I retorted, "we'll just have to call the project off!"

"I'm afraid that's impossible," the principal said. Apparently the project was already under way and some subscriptions had already been sold. Furthermore, the school had offered weekly prizes as a sales-boosting incentive and this had generated great enthusiasm among the students.

"Wonderful!" I commented sarcastically. "Now *chinuch* takes second place to high sales figures." I informed the principal that I was withdrawing my support for this project and hung up the phone.

Alone among all the board members in my disapproval, I allowed myself to feel properly self-righteous until one day when I found Devorah looking particularly unhappy. "What's wrong?" I asked.

"Oh, it's the stupid magazine sale," she replied. I correctly assessed "stupid" to mean the project in which I had disallowed her participation. "Every Tuesday during lunch period," she continued dejectedly, "they read off the number of magazines each kid sold and give out prizes. The principal always sends me to the library when they're doing this and I eat my sandwich there."

"What!" I exclaimed, appalled at what I saw as the principal's insensitivity in singling Devorah out like that.

"Oh, I don't really mind," she assured me unconvincingly. "The whole thing is so dumb anyway. But this week's prize is a giant chocolate bar with nuts and I'd really love to win *that*."

I didn't think trying to mollify my daughter by buying her the chocolate bar of her dreams was such a hot idea. A discussion on the subject of making sacrifices to uphold our principles would likewise not have gone very far in consoling her. So I simply let the matter lie and contemplated other potentially greater sacrifices my loved ones might be compelled to make in support of my high-minded principles. Did the gains really outweigh the losses? I wondered.

WHEN DAHVEED LEV, our second son, was born, Barbara and I wanted to have the *bris* in the Day School and to involve the students and their parents in the *mitzvah*. Still awe-struck by our miraculous and swift transition from despondent childlessness to joyful parenthood of, now, three delightful youngsters, we felt Dahveed Lev's *bris* was a very special *simchah* and we were happy to share it with the school. We were later shocked to learn that some parents had complained to the principal and the chairman of the Day School board; they maintained that a ceremony of this nature was too "violent and coarse" to involve small children. We refused to allow ill feelings to detract from our *simchah* and simply attributed it to communal ignorance. It was soon brought home to me, however, that the community did not have a monopoly in that area.

The year Devorah entered the fourth grade, the Day School organized a student choir. The enthusiasm of the boys and girls who were selected more than compensated for any deficiencies in natural talent. Under the guidance of a gifted young director, the choir mastered an impressive repertoire of Hebrew songs. Their performances at school functions and other local events brought smiles and an occasional tear to everyone who heard them. Soon the whole community began to take pride in these Jewish pupils. Their songs created a greater spirit of unity than any number of sermons, editorials or committee meetings could ever accomplish.

Devorah, as a member of the choir, looked forward to every rehearsal and performance and I, as a proud parent of a choir member, was one of its most ardent supporters. At its inception, I had asked several of the local rabbis about the propriety of boys and girls singing together and, while their responses varied, the general consensus was that the question of *kol isha* did not arise until after girls had reached *bas mitzvah* age. Some individuals felt that the entire issue of the suitability of girls singing publicly only pertained to occasions when they sang secular songs and did not arise when exclusively religious songs were performed.

As the school year continued, the choir received more and more invitations. Devorah brought home a mimeographed schedule of performances and when I looked it over, I noticed that a number of performances were to take place during *sefirah*, the seven-week period of semi-mourning between Pesach and Shavuos. I had learned that there are several reasons that this period in the Jewish calendar is regarded as one of serious contemplation tinged with sadness and remorse. One reason is that during this short space of time twelve thousand pairs of Rabbi Akiva's *talmidim* all died of plague because they failed to treat one another with proper respect. In later centuries many tragedies befell the Jewish people at this time of year, a fact which reminds us of the precariousness of our existence and our dependence on God for our well-being.

As a result of these considerations, a number of customs associated with mourning were adopted for this period. Haircutting, for example, is prohibited; wedding ceremonies do not take place, *and* people refrain from attending live musical events. Since I believed these injunctions to be so widely observed that they had taken on the status of laws, I couldn't understand how the director, an Orthodox Jew, had scheduled performances of the piano-accompanied choir during this period.

I approached the director, whose accomplishments I admired and valued, and asked him to explain the matter. He answered that, according to a particular rabbi he "held by", as long as the performances were devoted to religious music, it was permissible to schedule them during *sefirah*. I was a bit confused. "What do you mean when you say a particular rabbi you 'hold by'?" I asked, unfamiliar with this expression.

"There is one particular rabbi with whom I am very close," he explained. He had gotten to know the man when he had been a yeshivah student, and whenever he was unsure about some question he would ask the rabbi's advice. The choir director considered him to be his *rebbe* and would act according to his counsel.

As I listened to his reply, I realized that I had no such individual to whom I could readily turn. I didn't have the same depth of confidence or trust in any of the local rabbis who had been helpful to me in the past and I expected I'd find it difficult to accept their responses as sufficiently authoritative that I'd always be willing to be governed by their judgments. Increasingly, I was becoming aware of the fact that matters of Jewish law are not as black and white as I had first believed; just as Rabbi Fried had said, there are many greys and nuances. With no background of yeshivah learning, I was attempting to navigate the halachic seas without recourse to a reliable chart, and since I didn't have my own *rebbe*, I was also without a navigator, compass and sextant. My own ignorance, it seemed, knew no bounds.

I remembered that during one of our visits to Baltimore I had been very impressed by Rabbi Moshe Heinemann, *rav* of the Agudah synagogue. I also knew that he answered halachic questions, not only for the members of his community, but also for people who phoned him from outside of Baltimore. Barbara and I both agreed that I should call Rabbi Heinemann and ask his advice about the issue of the choir and *sefirah*.

After I explained the situation over the phone, Rabbi Heinemann asked for clarification. He specifically wanted to know what the consequences would be if Devorah did not participate in the musical programs during this period. I told him that the director had said that since the choir was a closely knit unit, her departure would undermine the cohesiveness of the group and she would therefore not be permitted to rejoin the choir. Rabbi Heinemann stated that while he personally believed it inappropriate to hold performances at that time, he felt it was best that I not do anything that would single Devorah out and thereby disrupt her schooling and affect her attitude toward learning.

From that point on, I found myself turning to Rabbi Heinemann on a number of occasions, since questions were always coming up. For example, when Devorah received an invitation to attend the birthday party of one of her classmates at a local non-kosher ice cream parlor, Rabbi Heinemann advised that she attend but refrain from eating. If we felt it necessary, he suggested, we could prepare some separate treats that Devorah could have while at the party.

As I came to rely on Rabbi Heinemann more and more, I became less acrimonious and shrill in my dealings with others. Still, there was much that continued to disturb me about the local Jewish establishment. My major mode of expression was through my weekly column in the local Jewish newspaper, and I had a seemingly endless supply of issues to write about.

WHILE I WAS frequently surprised at the attitude of the Jewish community on various issues, I was thoroughly unprepared for the outcry that followed one of my weekly columns. I had written an article in which I called on individuals not to attend weddings where one of the partners was not Jewish, moderating my position to exclude weddings of close relatives and those where the non-Jewish partner had been converted by any rabbi. I also called on the community to refrain from appointing to office in a Jewish organization any individual who was not Jewish or was married to a non-Jew. In the article, I argued that due to the public nature of weddings and organizational appointments, attendance at mixed-marriage ceremonies and endorsement of appointments of non-Jews (or spouses of non-Jews) to Jewish leadership positions constitute tacit approval of intermarriage.

I had not actually researched Jewish or halachic sources in formulating my position on this subject, nor had I discussed it with Rabbi Heinemann. I was merely voicing my own gut feelings and, I believed, those of many like-minded individuals in the community. I can't remember ever being more wrong.

The phone did not stop ringing. I received over one hundred strongly critical letters, some of them genuine "hate

Congregation Beth ▮▮▮▮
— FOUNDED 1789 —
1111 ▮▮▮ West ▮▮▮ Street ▮▮▮

2 February 1981

DR. ▮▮▮▮ RABBI

Dr. Allan M. Schwartzbaum
3615 Brook Road ▮▮▮▮▮

Dear Dr. Schwartzbaum:

Your column in the latest issue of "The Jewish News" was one of the most vicious and vitriolic I have ever read. I consider it completely legitimate for you to express your views in opposition to intermarriage. I am opposed to intermarriage also. But you went beyond the line of decency when you recommended your communal "ban" against rabbis who officiate at intermarriages. Your personal edicts were somewhat reminiscent of the Nuremberg Laws.

I do hope that no occasion arises for us to have anything to do with each other.

Sincerely,

Dear Editor:

Concerning the issue of The Jewish News, Januar▮ edition, my husband and I, along with our four ch▮ very much distressed at several articles.

1. The Aricle on "Intermarriage" by Dr. ▮ wartzbaum. I for one, did not convert prior to ou out of respect to my parents, although they wer▮ my religious sentiments were to the Jewish fa thoughts had been in my mind even before I r husband. As family loyalties, etc., are most ir Jewish faith, I am sure Dr. Schwartzbaum ca this.

Secondly, if friends and family (of the Jew supported us at our wedding in all differen▮ the marriage would still be intact.

Thirdly, before my conversion, I held s▮ in conservative sisterhoods, Hadassah, t▮ Jewish religious school and we have b▮ since they were of age for religious sch▮ my teenagers are most active in th▮ holding various offices and Gigi is no▮ Chairman for the Federation's camp▮

Dear Dr. Schwartzbaum:

Your "Viewpoint" on intermarriage in last weeks's Jewish News went beyond the boundaries of acceptablity. Urging community ostracism of those who intermarry is an ugly, anti-religious act.

No one is for intermarriage. Intermarriage and assimilation are serious problems in the world Jewish community, but there is no evidence to support the use of threatened retribution as a means of prevention. It has long been recognized that the threat of severe penal retribution has done little or nothing to prevent serious crime. Why should the threat of community social action do anything more than alienate and embitter those considering intermarriage?

I had always thought that the laws and practices of Judaism led to a life of ethics, morality and compassion. The advocacy of this schismatic and vicious "Code of Conduct" is no better than the self-righteous, exclusionary approach of the anti-Semite of the member of the Moral Majority. Jews have the responsibility to educate and embrace their children — to turn some of our children away is antithetical. Wouldn't it be better to teach them and help them and perhaps wind up with better Jewish families?

Your "Viewpoint" was offensive to me as a Jew and as a human being. I would not presume to ask for an apology, but I think it might be a good idea for you to seriously re-think your "Code" in terms of constructive, decent and human values.

Sincerely,
Sue ▮▮▮

mail". Behind the scenes, efforts were made to undermine my position in the university. What I had naively overlooked was the fact that my article had described a far more significant portion of the Jewish community than I had ever imagined, including one president of a women's organization and one executive officer of an influential agency. In fact, I had also unwittingly described the majority of the membership of the community's largest Reform synagogue.

One evening, during the height of the controversy, I took the phone off the hook to stop its incessant ringing. Barbara understood the strain I was suffering. "How are you holding up?" she asked sympathetically.

"Okay, I guess. Believe me, I never expected *this*. I must have really touched a raw nerve!"

"You know," Barbara went on, "I totally agree with everything you wrote, but at the same time I feel that all this altercation and discord is not really helping *us*. Sometimes I have the feeling you're a modern-day Jewish Don Quixote — instead of tilting at windmills, you're fighting assimilated Jews. I think it's time we began to work on *ourselves*, rather than trying to change the entire Jewish community at large."

As wrong as I had been in my assessment of public opinion, that's how right Barbara was about us. We had spent years gazing outward toward the broad horizons when we should have been peering in, examining and improving ourselves. It was time we readjusted our sights.

I began to reduce my involvement in local affairs and when I became eligible for a half-year sabbatical, I applied. After traveling around the world and living in many parts of it, we decided it was time to really go "home", home to the one place where we felt we could live our lives as complete Jews. We made reservations the very next day for our flight to *Eretz Yisrael*.

PART FIVE:

morning

Let us arise early in the morning
[and go] to the vineyards...

THE SONG OF SONGS 7:13

W E RENTED AN APARTMENT in the Jerusalem neighborhood of Ma'alot Daphna, near the Ohr Sameach Yeshiva where I intended to devote the six months of my sabbatical to learning full time. The apartment was very simple, and even a bit dilapidated, with sparse furnishings in various states of disrepair. A small *mirpeset* (outdoor porch) overlooked an open area — part park, part vacant lot — that led to the edge of the Shmuel Hanavi apartment complex, a low-income development which at one time had served as the border between Israel and her hostile neighbors. There was one small bedroom for Devorah, Dov Chaim and Dahveed Lev and another for Barbara and me. The kitchen, equipped with a tiny gas range, an antiquated refrigerator and narrow stone counters which were stained and cracked, boasted a small window with a spectacular view of the large metal trashbin in the yard. But the excitement and ebullience which Barbara and I felt upon our arrival in Israel transformed our surroundings into an idyll. In the early morning, sunshine streamed through the windows and enveloped everything in the dazzling, coruscating light of *Yerushalayim*.

The day after our arrival, I strode purposefully along the short blocks that separated our home from Ohr Sameach, my mind filled with thoughts of Rabbi Akiva. Like the Sage of old, I too was past forty years of age and was about to enroll in a yeshiva and learn Torah for the first time in my life. The propect was thrilling and terrifying at the same time.

RABBI YIRMIYAHU ABRAMOV,* who was responsible for new students, interviewed me and suggested a series of *shiurim* (classes) he thought appropriate. Together we worked out a schedule which would allow me to make the most of my relatively brief stay, and then I jumped right in.

My school day began with morning services, after which I attended a class on the laws pertaining to *teshuvah* (repentance). The class was taught by Rabbi Avigdor Bonchek, who was also a practicing clinical psychologist. I found the insights provided by Maimonides in his works on this subject to be utterly fascinating, and amazingly timely.

After a brief break, there was a *Gemara shiur* on Tractate Sanhedrin, led by Rabbi Ely Merl, and after lunch, classes on *Mishnah* and *Chumash*. In the evenings, I reviewed the *Gemara shiur* with my *chavrusa*, a more advanced student who was paired with me as a study partner, and at ten P.M. I attended one of the regularly scheduled evening lectures on a wide range of subjects. I particularly relished Rabbi Mordechai Perlman's analyses of *parshas ha-shavua* (the weekly portion of the Torah) and Rabbi Dovid Gottlieb's discussions of various philosophical issues.

As much as I enjoyed the total program, it was the *Gemara* that most excited me. I had never experienced anything like it in all my years of academic research and scholarship. My discovery of Judaism had been, up to this point, a voyage into uncharted waters. But when I first opened my *Gemara*, I felt I was undertaking a new and altogether different sort of voyage, this time in search of hidden treasure. Since compre-

* In this section I have used the actual names of the rabbis, teachers and other personalities with whom I came in contact. They contributed substantially to my religious development and are worthy not only of my acknowledgment, but of my heartfelt gratitude as well.

hension was proportional to one's mental effort, I was now not merely a passive passenger but a vital member of the crew.

The *Mishnah* was the point of embarkation. In very terse and compact language, the *Mishnah* presented a set of principles in what might have been called in university jargon a "position statement". Crafted with precision, the *Mishnah* served as the core document. Written in a code of its own, it served as a map — a treasure map — providing clues and guidelines. What lay ahead was the actual expedition.

One begins by following the leads of the *Mishnah* down a particular channel, only to discover that others have already traveled this route, leaving behind a log of their findings in the form of a *beraisa*. So one sets off again in another direction, periodically referring to the *Mishnah*'s map in order not to wander too far afield. Everything can serve as a signpost or clue; a particular phrase, grammar, spelling — all enter into the search. There are numerous ports of call along the way. The most interesting and brilliant characters, including the greatest of our Sages, embark at various stages in the journey.

There were many points where I was hopelessly at sea. Fortunately, there were a number of invaluable navigational charts available, especially those prepared by Rashi and *Ba'alei Ha-tosefos*. I eventually realized that although there was a final destination in the form of a conclusion and in some cases a point of law, or *halachah*, what mattered more was the journey itself and not the destination. The riches were not to be found in some hidden treasure trove concealed in a cave or buried beneath the ocean. The jewels were meant to be gathered along the way. The penetrating insights, the relentless pursuit of a clean line of reason, the extravagant Talmudic discussions taken together revealed a way of life based on Torah principles.

For me, the *Gemara* represented the greatest intellectual challenge I had ever encountered. My graduate and doctoral work were minor swells to the Talmud's majestic waves. I realized for the first time the monolithic nature of Jewish learning: a proper understanding of any single section presumed an understanding of the total body of Torah knowledge. There was no beginning and no end. A *Gemara* discussion could weave its way throughout all of Torah; a thread of thought would be reinforced by citing a particular *pasuk*, or phrase, in one of the five books of the Bible, or by quoting from one of the Proverbs or Psalms, or by referring to a section in the Prophets. The more one searched, the more one discovered; the greater the discovery, the greater the urge to search even further.

My Torah studies filled my days, my evenings, my nights; my hunger for learning was insatiable. The yeshiva provided a spiritual sustenance unparalleled by any other educational environment in my experience. I was particularly impressed by the *chavrusa* system of learning, wherein each student is paired with a study partner. The *beis midrash*, or study hall, of a yeshiva is populated by these study pairs who, oblivious to the din of their surroundings, review the day's *shiur*, grappling with the complicated and intricate web of ideas and positions which fill each page of the *Gemara*.

The partners often adopt confrontational postures, arguing forcibly for their own interpretations and seeking to find flaws and inconsistencies in their associate's viewpoint. To an outsider, this war of words might appear to be tinged with impatience, irritation and exasperation. To the participants, however, there is mutual respect, deep appreciation and, often, the development of a long-lasting friendship. Like two blades scraping against each other, the minds of the study partners are honed to ever-increasing sharpness.

The *chavrusa* system works best when the two partners are well-matched in temperament and intellectual skills. Ideally, there should be a complementarity of strengths and weaknesses. The most obvious analogy would be to a marriage: here the *rebbeim* play a key role in matchmaking but, just as in marriage, there is no such thing as a "perfect spouse". Every *chavrusa* has to learn to live with his study partner's idiosyncrasies.

I found the principle that one has a responsibility for another student's success in learning to be remarkably enlightened and in sharp contradistinction to the rampant competition and one-upmanship which characterizes the secular world. Even more remarkable was the fact that individuals appear for class and devote long hours to study outside of class without any externally imposed system of reward and punishment: there are no grades, no exams, no diplomas, no awards. Students learn in yeshivos because they want to, because they find the material intrinsically exciting and meaningful, because they consider it their religious obligation and privilege, and not simply because their parents want them to learn. In fact, as I got to know my classmates better, I realized that in many cases their parents were anything but supportive.

THE AVERAGE AGE of my fellow students was twenty-two. At forty-two, I was one of a handful of "senior citizens" learning in the yeshiva, and as such was periodically called upon to offer advice and counsel. A recurring problem among the students was parental opposition to their newly-adopted lifestyle. Frequently this opposition took the form of pressure to leave Israel in order to continue formal secular studies in college or university.

Although I was unable to provide simple answers or formulas for dealing with such issues, I always stressed that no matter how seemingly deep and wide the divergence in views, one must remain respectful and attempt to see things from the parents' perspective. I suggested that when a son dramatically and radically altered his way of life, his belief system, his values, his activities, even his attire in ways that were fundamentally different from the way of life followed by his parents, it was understandable for his mother and father to interpret this as an implicit rebuke and rejection of the way they raised him. Bruised feelings seemed inevitable. When one added the fact that thousands of miles separated them, it was easy to see how parents might be genuinely worried about their children.

Privately, I felt that the rapid rate of change, the almost overnight metamorphosis from a hippie-like continent-hopping college student to a conservatively dressed *yeshiva bachur* with *tzitzis* conspicuously displayed was in some cases too sudden and abrupt, and that these external transformations had outpaced the internal revisions and adjustments which were still in progress. The "before" and "after" appearance of their offspring was occasionally emotionally overwhelming to parents who were struggling to deal with the new direction their child's life had taken.

Whatever concerns I entertained about the students from Western countries, however, did not apply to individuals in the yeshiva's Israeli section. I observed in amazement their almost instantaneous changeover and reformation. Exposed throughout their lives to the unique history, language and atmosphere which permeates the Land of Israel, yet deprived of active and meaningful participation, the secular Israelis were like dry kindling waiting to be ignited. The moment they were touched by a spark of Torah, they virtually burst into flame. As they prayed and learned, their enthusiasm and ardor singed all those around them.

The question of how yeshiva students should approach their secular college studies and future careers was a complex one. I knew first hand from my many years as a college student and university professor that the campus could be a particularly ill-suited environment for shaping the lives of young people. While universities are forums for the exchange of views, where dedicated individuals probe the physical and natural world, and where students can sample and study the best in art, music and literature and observe great minds at work, these opportunities are presented in a setting of frivolous abandonment of responsibility. Young impressionable students, free for the first time of parental restriction, encounter relaxed norms which allow permissive sexual behavior and experimentation with drugs. They are confronted with a bewildering variety of student subgroups they have never interacted with before. It is an environment that in many ways is antithetical to Torah values. Still, I am a product of this environment. Although I had emerged more or less intact and came away with an appreciation of science, humanities and research, many were far less fortunate. From my present perspective I can see the countless pitfalls, but do these necessarily preclude any pursuit of higher education?

The more I considered this question, the more convinced I became that there was no inherent contradiction between the secular and religious worlds. The atomic structure of particles, the complex symbolism of linguistic systems, the intricate rhythms of a Bach fugue, the movement of tides and the earth's crust, the migratory patterns of birds, illustrated the infinity and awesome wisdom of God. Secular studies were a window into heaven and an entranceway to Torah.

What was necessary, I concluded, was first to be rooted in a Torah perspective. The sequence I had followed — first completing my secular studies and then, years later, going to yeshiva — was fraught with danger. How many of my classmates had fallen by the wayside? How many, although materially successful, seemed to be disenchanted, adrift and listless? How many were neither successful nor disenchanted but had "tuned in, turned on and dropped out"? It was almost absurd to think that *these* individuals would ever find themselves in a yeshiva. After "breaking my teeth" daily over the *Gemara*, I had come to realize how difficult it was to catch up. There was only one Rabbi Akiva. Few — if any — who have had such a late start could become one of Judaism's greatest Sages.

What disturbed me, however, was what I sensed to be an unfair and distorted disparagement of secular knowledge by some representatives of the yeshiva world. During the period I was in the yeshiva, a controversy was raging in Jerusalem over the disturbance of ancient grave sites as a result of archeological excavations in the Old City. A noted speaker addressed the yeshiva on this issue. He reviewed the Jewish approach to death which is founded on the sacredness of man. He compared a human being with a Torah scroll that, if impaired, can no longer be used for ritual purposes. Nonetheless, the scroll continues to be revered for the exalted role it once filled. Man is created in the image of God; the human form is not a mere empty shell, a collection of skeletal remains, a source of data, but something that must be respected for having once embodied the spirit of God. Disinterment, except for clearly-specified, exceptional circumstances, is a disgrace to the deceased.

I saw the wisdom of this approach and knew from my many travels that a society's attitude toward its dead was one of the surest indications of its attitude toward the living. But the speaker carried his theme further and began to vehemently assail anthropology, which he portrayed as a field whose teachings were diametrically opposed to Torah.

At the conclusion of the discourse, I addressed the speaker. "I appreciate the worth of what you've told us this evening," I said, "but I believe that it is inappropriate to condemn all anthropology, to render an entire field and discipline *'treif'* and to depict it as totally devoid of any redeeming value." This was, after all, a subject that was rather close to my heart.

"First," I went on, "anthropology consists of numerous subfields. Archeology, which is the focus of the activities which have disturbed the sanctity of the ancient Jewish tombs, is only one anthropological specialization among many. Second, I believe that a Torah Jew can use the insights and knowledge provided by anthropology in ways that do not violate Torah, in ways that will benefit man. There is no inevitable conflict with Torah. For example, anthropology has a great deal to teach us about the successful utilization and management of resources. It can inform us about how culture interacts with ecological factors, thereby encouraging or discouraging adaptation to the environment. It can help us understand the socialization process and the dynamics by which the older generation transfers its culture to a newer generation. It can help us promote inter-group cooperation by providing examples of cross-cultural understanding. We shouldn't condemn anthropology, but rather the way certain anthropologists practice anthropology."

"Yes," the speaker conceded. "You could also say that television has the potential to do a certain amount of good." And with that, he turned to the next questioner.

I found this grudging, backhanded acknowledgment of my position to be highly unsatisfactory and disquieting. I continued to grapple with the issues involved until I eventually reached a partial resolution that satisfied my own need to reconcile the secular with the spiritual. I recalled that most universities have a School of Arts and a School of Sciences. This traditional organization of academic subjects into the Arts, which normally embodies humanistic studies such as philosophy, literature, language, music and art, and the Sciences, which includes both the physical and natural sciences, suggests a key distinction.

The Arts or Humanities stresses the relativeness of human conduct and endeavor. Tastes, fashions, ethics, values, all vary with the historical epoch, the prevailing socioeconomic conditions, and ongoing cultural exchanges. Societies, with their critics and spokesmen, serve as the arbiters of what is good, beautiful, just and deserving. There are no eternal standards, only emergent criteria. There is no place for an omnipresent Creator whose transcendent, unvarying wisdom guides man. Great art and literature is seen as a product of individual genius.

This genius, however, has its origins in God's gift to the artist. The Torah says, "I have selected Bezalel son of Uri, son of Chur, of the tribe of Yehudah, by name. I have filled him with a Divine spirit, with wisdom, understanding and knowledge, and with the talent for all types of craftsmanship" (*Shemos* 31:2,3). Unless the artist acknowledges this debt, the works fashioned by his hand become idols glorifying what man has created, rather than offerings praising the Creator of man.

Scientists, however, do not create; they detect. They have an openness born of exploration and discovery. They do not fabricate mysteries; they uncover them. I found a reference* citing the *Midrash Rabbah* on *Eichah* 2:13, which seemed to represent this distinction: "As our Sages said, 'If someone tells you there is science among the other nations, believe him; Torah among the other nations, do not believe him.'"

There are some fields which do not fall neatly into one category or the other. The Social Sciences, such as anthropology, sociology and psychology, occupy a nebulous intermediate point between the sciences and the humanities. These disciplines have become increasingly scientific. Their interpretations and recommendations, however, often hover somewhere between the empirically generated findings and the personal values and ideology of the researcher. Engineering is also difficult to place. The phenomenal achievements in these fields are often accompanied by a technical arrogance which seems to inflate the role of man in this world. Here, too, as in the Humanities, it is the element of personal vanity which can change an innocuous or potentially beneficial discipline into a "*treif*" one. Possibly, if one approaches an area of secular study with a firmly-grounded Torah perspective, the risk of falling prey to that arrogance is minimized. Possibly, this statement in itself is tinged with arrogance.

As I said, I considered this no more than a partial resolution.

* "Torah and Secular Studies: The Humanities," by Leo Levi, *Proceedings of the Associations of Orthodox Jewish Scientists*, vol. v, 1979.

WHILE I WAS learning at Ohr Sameach, Dov Chaim went to *cheder* in the nearby Sanhedria Murchevet neighborhood, Dahveed stayed with a *metapelet* who looked after children in her home, and Barbara took courses at Neve Yerushalayim* and studied Hebrew. Devorah attended fourth grade at a Bais Yaakov elementary school.

It was Devorah who had the most difficult time adjusting. Back in America, where the Asian population is far from negligible and where, even in the Jewish communities, there are plenty of children whose features resembled Devorah's (either adopted children or the offspring of American servicemen and their Korean or Vietnamese wives), she had not been an oddity. In Israel, however, she stood out as sharply as blonde Dov Chaim had in Taiwan, and was the object of far more attention than she would have liked. The difference was that Dov Chaim had been too young to notice the staring and the Chinese people had been, for the most part, too polite to make any untoward remarks.

Devorah was almost ten years old and for the first time in her young life was made to feel like a freak. Total strangers felt no qualms about challenging her Jewishness and her

* A women's seminary with a program for students with limited background in Judaic studies.

right to be in the Jewish holy land; children mocked and abused her; even her teachers at times seemed unable to cope with a situation that deviated from their concept of the norm. Barbara and I were frequently reduced to tears ourselves as we dried our daughter's eyes and tried to help her to understand prejudice, bigotry, insensitivity and a few other marvels of a cold, cruel world. We felt certain — or at least hopeful — that all would be well once Devorah made new friends and gained more self-assurance.

DEVORAH'S STRUGGLES struck the only sour note in what was otherwise the sweetest symphony we'd ever known. Barbara and I were "high" on Israel and as time passed, Jerusalem began more and more to seep into our bones. We would walk everywhere, through all the neighborhoods, the side streets and alleyways. While in America our Sabbaths and Jewish holidays were occasional interludes in the cycle of work, school and leisure, in Jerusalem they were the high points of a continuous spiritual involvement. The first time I heard the sirens sounded throughout the city heralding the onset of Shabbos, my hair stood on end.

"You know," I told Barbara, "in America a Jew is always temporally out of phase. Jewish time is not synchronized to the life of the city or neighborhood. Jewish and gentile life follow different rhythms. It's just one more distinction between 'us' and 'them'. When we kept Shabbos, we created a small island for ourselves surrounded by a sea of people mowing their lawns, playing their stereos, driving their cars. Here Shabbos is on Shabbos."

Barbara agreed. "I know exactly what you mean. When we were living in the States, I felt that no matter how hard we tried to lift ourselves up spiritually, the surroundings would pull us down. Here, no matter how personally inadequate we are, the surroundings pull us up."

Thus, without ever really stating it openly, Barbara and I both knew we had reached a decision: we were going to live and raise our children in Israel.

The first positive step I took in this direction was to open a file with the Ministry of Absorption. The ministry had a special department to assist academics seeking to immigrate to Israel. Over the next few months I was interviewed at the four major Israeli universities and a number of other institutions and agencies, but nothing concrete developed from these contacts. It was very disheartening. With no serious prospects for a livelihood in sight, it looked as though our resolve to make *Aliyah* would crumble.

When only weeks remained until the end of my sabbatical period, a friend suggested we speak to Rebbetzin Esther Segal, a woman known for her extraordinary acts of *chessed*. At certain times each day individuals came to seek her advice and receive her *berachah*. We had no idea of how she might help us, but a *berachah* from a saintly woman certainly couldn't hurt.

BARBARA AND I walked from Ma'alot Daphna to Meah Shearim and found Rebbetzin Segal's small unassuming house behind a small alley adjacent to the Mirrer Yeshiva. The rebbetzin greeted us and offered us a cool drink and some fruit before we began and we gratefully accepted. Barbara then related a little about our background, our gradual development and growth in *Yiddishkeit*, and our concern about returning to the United States. I spoke of my futile efforts to find work. Once told, our tale of woe seemed embarrassingly inconsequential and we both shifted a bit uncomfortably in our seats. But the rebbetzin treated our situation with utmost seriousness.

"For your children's welfare," she said, "it is vital that you leave your old community as soon as possible and return quickly to *Eretz Yisrael*." Then, looking directly at me, she continued, "I believe your problem is that you feel you must be in complete control of the situation at all times. You are not ready to do anything unless you believe that everything is in place and that you can regulate and direct the situation. You must realize, however, that none of us controls anything. *HaKadosh Baruch Hu* determines what happens to us, He makes things occur, He restrains things."

She waited for that to sink in before she went on. "Until you accept that, until you develop true *emunah*, faith in *Hashem*, you will not be able to progress. The first step is to recognize that it is God, not you, who is in control. You still must do everything you can, of course — you would not cross the street with your eyes closed and say 'God will take care of everything' — but remember, in the end things are not in your own hands. Look around — everyone seems to be eating, no one is sleeping in the street. People manage. If you want to stay here, you must trust in *Hashem*."

THANKING REBBETZIN SEGAL, we took our leave and began walking slowly back to our apartment. We had walked about halfway in silence, each of us lost in private thoughts, when we came upon a sidewalk bench and stopped for a moment to rest. I turned to Barbara and said, "Everything was so simple and plain. Her house was completely unadorned, no frills at all — but spotless, and her manner very much suited her home — austere, almost severe. Yet despite the simplicity, I sensed something a little out of the ordinary. Did you feel it too?"

Barbara nodded. "But how did you feel about what she had to say? She seemed to be talking directly to you."

I replayed a mental recording of the rebbetzin's words in my head. After a lengthy pause I said, "I think the lady has got my number."

ALL TOO QUICKLY, my sabbatical came to an end. We packed our belongings, said our goodbyes, and returned to the United States. So distant and insulated had we been from the "goyish" world that, until our plane landed, we were unaware that our arrival would coincide with the peak of the winter holiday season. The ubiquitous ornaments and decorations, the inescapable jingles, the frenetic tumult in the malls and on the sidewalks assaulted our senses, contrasting sharply with the quiet tranquility of Jerusalem. Some of our Jewish neighbors had begun erecting their "Chanukah bushes," as they did every year; this time it was simply too much for us.

Within a few weeks, we put our home up for sale. Although I had no job possibilities lined up elsewhere, Barbara and I agreed we could no longer remain in our present environment. We made a tentative decision to move to Baltimore where we knew there was a thriving and growing observant Jewish community and to retain my current job until I could find a new position. It would mean long separations and commuting to Baltimore each weekend in order to spend Shabbos with the family, but we were certain the sacrifice would be worthwhile. Our brief taste of living among Jews like ourselves made us hunger for more.

THOUSANDS OF YEARS ago, the Sabbath before the very first Pesach in Egypt fell on the tenth of Nissan. It has been known through the millennia as *"Shabbos Ha-gadol"*, for on that day the Children of Israel performed their first *mitzvah*: preparing a lamb for the Pesach offering. Great and miraculous events occurred on that day, including, in the year 5742, the birth of our third son.

His arrival five days before Pesach presented us with an immediate predicament: the eighth day after his birth, the day on which the *bris* was to take place, would be the following Shabbos, the seventeeth of Nissan. With no *mohel* available locally, someone would have to come from out-of-town to perform the *bris*, but he'd have to be willing to arrive before *erev Yom Tov* — Wednesday — and stay through the two days of *Yom Tov* and Shabbos! We couldn't imagine anyone agreeing to spend the first three days of Pesach, including the *sedarim*, away from his family.

On Tuesday evening after I brought Barbara home from the hospital, I phoned Rabbi Yehudah Naftali Mandelbaum, a teacher in She'aris Ha-pleita Talmud Torah in Baltimore. Although we had known the Mandelbaums for only a very brief time, having enjoyed Chanukah with them upon our return from Israel, I felt confident that Rabbi Mandelbaum would be able to resolve our dilemma. I explained the problem and, to my astonishment, Rabbi Mandelbaum — without a moment's hesitation — invited us all to spend Pesach with his family. He told me not to worry about anything: we'd have the *sedarim* at his home, and he would make arrangements for the *bris* on Shabbos.

The next day, Wednesday, we piled into our small car, Devorah alongside me in the front, and Barbara, Dahveed, Dov and the new baby in the back. We arrived at the Mandelbaums' around two P.M. and Mrs. Mandelbaum, who was expecting her seventh child, made us feel immediately at home, as if it were the most natural thing in the world to have two adults, three children and a newborn as Pesach guests with one day's notice.

On Friday night, there was a double *shalom zachar*: ours and the Perkals', the Mandelbaums' neighbors across the street who also had a new baby boy. It seemed that the whole city turned out for the double *simchah* and for the *bris* the following day. Rabbi Heineman, *rav* of the Agudas Yisrael Synagogue, was the *sandak*, and Rabbi Moshe Rappaport was the *mohel*. On the seventeenth of Nissan, Shmuel Naftali Schwartzbaum entered the Covenant of Abraham.

On Sunday morning, after thanking the Mandelbaums over and over again for all they had done, we left for home. The hospitality shown us by the Orthodox community had left a deep impression and I was more convinced than ever that we should move to Baltimore as soon as possible. It was clearly a better environment in which to raise our children, a place where they could get proper schooling and would have plenty of friends. Shmuel Naftali *already* had a common bond with one Baltimorean — the Perkals' baby!

When we got home, I glanced at the mail that had accumulated over the past few days and found among the bills, notices and personal letters an envelope from the American Zionist Federation. I made a mental note to look at it at the first opportunity, and then went to help Barbara get the children settled after their long trip.

It wasn't until after eleven o'clock that night that I had a chance to examine the letter. It read: "The State University of New York has had a branch in Jerusalem, Israel for a number of years. We have recently received word from the Ministry of Immigrant Absorption in Jerusalem that the Student Authority and the Center for Absorption in Science will give money to cover the expenses of an additional faculty member for the program in Jerusalem. A principle of the agreement is that the faculty member must come to Israel as a new immigrant."

I read and reread the letter, amazed at having the answer to our prayers fall right in our lap. Barbara agreed that this was the ideal solution for us so, on the spot, I applied for the position. "It's really strange," I remarked. "When we were still in Israel, I registered with the Ministry of Absorption but they never said a word about this job. Now, here we are, back in America, and almost by accident a friend of a friend mentions my name, and the American Zionist Federation sends me the notice!"

"First of all," Barbara replied, "*nothing* happens by accident. And second of all, I think we had to *leave* Israel in order to realize how important it was for us to *return*."

From that point on things moved very quickly. I was invited to New York for an interview and within a month's time was offered the post for the coming spring semester. On January 18, 1983, we arrived back at Ben Gurion Airport, a little more than one year after we had left *Eretz Yisrael*. This time, however, we were not just visitors; we were immigrants, assigned to the absorption center in Gilo, in the south of Jerusalem.

With a rising sense of adventure and tremendous enthusiasm, we completed the necessary paperwork and indicated that henceforth our names should be recorded as Avraham and Rochel. We had exchanged our three-story, six-bedroom house in the United States for two rooms in an absorption center in Gilo, and our hearts sang.

I T WAS ONLY a year to Devorah's *bas mitzvah* and Rochel and I recognized that this was to be an important milestone for her, more so than for other Jewish girls. She had been converted as a child of four, an age when she could not possibly have been expected to make a reasoned, independent decision about becoming Jewish; upon coming of age halachically, Devorah would have the opportunity to make that decision on her own. She could, if she so desired, nullify the conversion and revert to her former status as a non-Jew.

We had no idea what procedures or ceremonies, if any, were required in order for Devorah to reaffirm her Jewish status, and we were especially anxious that there be no question whatsoever about the validity of her conversion. This was particularly important in Israel, where an individual's right to marry was contingent upon the validation and verification of one's Jewish status to the satisfaction of the Chief Rabbinate.

There was another issue which concerned me. Devorah was not only a convert; she was also an adopted child. This raised a set of additional questions with regard to her coming of age, and I read as much as I could on this subject.

I was familiar with the statement in *Sanhedrin* 19b that "whosoever rears an orphan in his own house is considered by Scripture as if he fathered the child." I also knew that the evidence for adoption in *Tanach* was so ambiguous and equivocal that most commentators denied the existence of the practice. There are references to Avraham's relationship to Eliezer, his servant, and his statement that Eliezer will be his heir; Bitiah's actions in saving and rearing Moshe; Mordechai's custodianship of Esther; the allusion to Ruth's child as the son of Naomi; and Michal, the daughter of King Saul, raising the children of her sister Meirav. While occasionally cited as cases of adoption, these references have all been shown to be at most examples of fosterage.

I learned that according to Jewish law, the relationship of natural parent and child is unique, and cannot be artificially duplicated. Thus, even though an adoption creates a legal relationship which imposes certain responsibilities on both the new parent and the child, it never replaces true consanguinity nor alters the blood relationship between the adoptee and his or her biological parents. Should the adopted child smite or curse his adoptive parents, he is not subject to the severe punishment set down in the Torah for a child acting this way toward his natural parents. All forbidden incestual relationships apply only to relatives by nature, not by adoption. Thus, the Torah does not forbid a marriage between an adoptee and her adoptive parents' biological children, although the Rabbis actively discourage such a bond. In addition, the status of *Kohain* or *Levi* is not transmitted from adoptive father to adopted child.

These rulings did not appear to me to have any practical consequences for us, until I chanced upon a statement by the Lubavitcher Rebbe about the issue of *yichud ve-kiruv basar*. Referring to the Jewish laws forbidding physical contact and seclusion between an unrelated man and woman, the Lubavitcher Rebbe raised what he considered to be the analogous problem of seclusion and kissing and hugging between adopted children and their adoptive parents. Suddenly I wondered about my own relationship with Devorah and what was permitted and what was not. I decided to seek the advice of Rabbi Naftali Lewin, the rabbi assigned to the local absorption centers.

When I met Rabbi Lewin, I was impressed by his quiet, thoughtful manner, his sincerity and his obvious erudition. I told him a bit about our background and then presented the questions relating to Devorah's *bas mitzvah.* "Does she have to go to the *mikveh* again? Is it necessary for her to make any public avowal of her decision to remain Jewish? Do we need witnesses? Is a new certificate of conversion written at that time?" I asked. "And what about my relationship with my daughter? Are we allowed to touch? What will happen when her brothers reach maturity?"

Despite his familiarity with the subject, Rabbi Lewin was reluctant to offer his opinion, a fact I considered a lesson in itself. "In order to make sure that everything is one hundred percent," he said, " we should consult a recognized authority, a renowned *poseik* who can provide clear answers to all your questions. Fortunately, I know such a *poseik* — Rabbi Shlomo Zalman Auerbach, the dean of the Kol Torah Yeshiva. He is one of the leading *posekim* in the world I will make an appointment for you to see him and accompany you, if you like." He wrote down his phone number t home and asked that I call him in three days' time.

ON THE APPOINTED DAY, I arrived at Rabbi Lewin's office in Binyanei Ha-uma opposite the Central Bus Sta ion. Together we proceeded to Rav Shlomo Zalman's house in the residential neighborhood of Sha'arei Chessed. There, on a quiet side street, we climbed a flight of stone teps to the Rav's home. We had only a brief wait in ide before being invited into his study.

I felt an immediate affinity for the elderly distinguished-looking rabbi seated behind a table laden with books. There was a special quality to his appearance, a mixture of integrity and strength, warmth and kindness. His eyes were active

and alive — the eyes of a young man. Rabbi Lewin introduced me and then, in a combination of Hebrew and Yiddish, related our history and my questions.

Rabbi Auerbach listened carefully and responded in a
soft but firm voice. "If a child has been continuously
engaged in keeping *mitzvos* since conversion, there is no
need to do anything special. If on the twelfth birthday plus
one day in the case of a girl, and on the thirteenth birthday
plus one day in the case of a boy, the child, aware that he or
she was converted and has the option of rejecting Judaism,
nevertheless continues in the usual manner to be *shomer
mitzvos*, the conversion becomes complete and permanent.
There is no need for a verbal declaration; there is no need for
witnesses. If the individual wishes to make an affirmation,
that is acceptable, but not required by *halachah*. Again, this
presumes a continuity of behavior.

"If, on the other hand, the individual chooses to
renounce Judaism, he or she must verbally reject the conversion and engage in an act which violates Jewish law. If he or
she begins to demonstrate non-Jewish behavior — for example, eating *'treif'* food or violating Shabbos — and this act is
done with the intent of rejecting Judaism, the conversion is
nullified."

The Rabbi paused a moment to allow me to absorb this
information, then continued: "Now, regarding the laws
governing physical contact, isolation and seclusion —
yichud with your daughter should not present much of a
practical problem, since you and your wife live in the same
house and there are currently a number of small children
who reside there as well. A question of *yichud* might arise
under special circumstances, but there are always arrangements one can make with neighbors to stay over, or similar
solutions to eliminate the problem.

"*Negiah*, or physical contact, only refers to that associated with expressions of affection. We are not considering
any contact that comes about as a result of routine, normal

chores or activities, such as passing objects from one person to the other. It is also important to know that in all religious households there is a natural lessening of physical contact between fathers and their daughters as the daughters grow older."

I myself had noticed this, not only in religious households but in non-religious and even non-Jewish households, although to a lesser degree. There were sociological and psychological reasons for this behavior pattern, I knew, and once again I was struck by the far-reaching wisdom of the Sages. The legislation of *halachos* clearly reflected a firm grasp of the immutable truths of life and a deep understanding of the human psyche.

I nodded my agreement and Rabbi Auerbach went on: "The considerations of *negiah* will also apply to your natural sons when they pass the age of nine. You should do everything with common sense. I know of one very esteemed rabbi who blesses his daughters-in-law on Shabbos and does not worry about placing his hands on their heads, as is customary, when he offers the blessing.

"Everything I have said assumes the child's awareness of his or her status as an adoptee and convert. It is very important to apprise the child of this status, otherwise she may wish to marry a *Kohain*, who is halachically forbidden to marry her."

The *Rav*, having completed his response, blessed me and my family, that we should settle easily in *Eretz Yisrael*, that our adjustment to a new life should not be too difficult, and that our love and knowledge of Torah should grow stronger and deeper each year.

I thanked him for his blessing, left the study and walked down the stone stairs while Rabbi Lewin remained behind to have a few last words with Rav Shlomo Zalman. Waiting for him to rejoin me, I reviewed Rabbi Auerbach's *psak* in my mind, staring unseeingly at the traffic on the street. The *Rav* had addressed my reason — the rational part of me that

collected and sorted data — and I had responded in a reasoned, rational fashion, but now my emotions came into
play. Rabbi Lewin suddenly appeared at my side and
remarked on my pensive mood. "You seem very quiet and a
bit sad," he said. "Is there anything wrong?"

"I was just thinking," I replied, "that I won't be able to
touch my daughter anymore, not even to kiss her goodnight
or goodbye."

I WAITED UNTIL all the children were asleep before relating
to Rochel the outcome of my meeting with Rabbi Auerbach.
"He was very nice," I told her. "I felt I was in the presence of
someone special. I had to listen very carefully to every word
he said, because every word carried a message. At first I didn't
understand why he mentioned this rabbi who *bentched* his
daughters-in-law on Shabbos, but now I see that what he was
trying to do was to put this whole business of physical
contact into perspective. He had tremendous sensitivity. And
by reminding me of the normal lessening of physical contact
in a natural father-daughter relationship, he reassured me
that the practical consequences of my situation would not be
so difficult to bear."

Rochel, who knows me so well, sensed that I was troubled
by what I had learned. She listened quietly while I thought it
all out aloud, working out for myself what she seemed to
know intuitively. "You know, Rochel, what really bothers
me is not so much the *halachah*; I can accept that. In fact, I
think after all is said and done, Rabbi Auerbach was right —
it really won't be so difficult. First of all, we are talking about
a father and daughter. It would probably be a lot harder for a
mother and an adopted son, since mothers tend to display
more overt affection, more mothering. And second, my own
personality is more or less suited to this situation. I'm not so
much the huggy-touchy type. I tend to be more reserved."

"So what is bothering you, then?" she asked softly, knowing I was rationalizing.

"What I don't understand," I continued, "is why in all these years no one ever mentioned these things to us. We have been *shomrei mitzvos* now for more than seven years. All the rabbis we've associated with knew that Devorah isn't our biological child — all they had to do was look at her. But no one ever said a word. I had to discover all this by myself. *I* had to come up with the questions. *I* had to go and find answers. And it's not as though our situation is so unique. Even when people remarry, the same questions arise with respect to the stepchildren from a former marriage. Why did no one say anything to us about it?"

"Avraham, I think it *is* the *halachah* that's bothering you, but let's put that aside for a moment. The rabbis didn't warn us about this for a very simple reason: they thought we weren't ready to accept such a thing, and frankly, I don't think they were wrong. Look, you said it yourself: we've been observant for over seven years. We should by now be able to learn and accept *halachos* that are new for us without making a fuss, don't you think? And yet you're still getting upset about this matter. How would you have reacted if one of the rabbis had told you this when we were just starting out? You might have become so worked up that it would somehow have set us back." She waited for me to digest this before giving me the clincher.

"*Hashem* doesn't present anyone with a problem until He thinks he can handle it," she said soothingly. "The fact is that today we learned the *halachah*. This demonstrates just how far we've come, since *Hashem* must think you and I are now capable of dealing with it."

I looked up at my wife — this wise woman who shared my life and my thoughts, who all along the way had seemed so much surer than I — and couldn't help but smile. She possessed a deep reserve of inner strength and whenever problems arose, she simply reached down and hauled out the wherewithal to deal with them. I knew then we'd weather this storm together, as we had weathered so many storms in the past.

THE TIME of Devorah's *bas mitzvah* was drawing near and Rochel and I wanted to share the *simchah* with our parents. Since the trip was too difficult for them to undertake, a week before Devorah's birthday we traveled to the United States. All my mother's friends and neighbors at the Jewish senior citizens' apartment complex in Orlando were invited to join in our celebration, which was to take place there. Rochel's parents came down from New York and a number of our other relatives flew in for the occasion. Everyone gathered in the main auditorium of the complex. The room became hushed as Devorah moved to the stage and addressed the assembled:

"Often when someone becomes a *bas* or *bar mitzvah*, they try to travel to Israel to commemorate the event. I have come from Israel to Florida so that I could be with my grandparents who, along with my parents, have helped and guided me through my first twelve years.

"For every Jewish girl, turning twelve is something special; it's something every Jewish girl looks forward to. But because I was adopted and converted as a small child, becoming twelve is extra special. In my case, I am able to decide whether or not I want to remain Jewish. I can make my own decision. My parents told me when I was very young that when I turned twelve I would have to make this decision on my own. I remember when I was small and I wanted to get back at my parents for not letting me have my own way, I would yell, 'I'm not going to stay Jewish when I'm twelve, just because of you!'

"Well, that time has finally come, and I don't even have to *think* about my decision. I want to remain Jewish. I can't think of any other way of life. I feel a special *kesher*, a connection with *bnei Yisrael*. When the Festivals come, I grow excited. On Shabbos I feel different. On Rosh Hashanah and Yom Kippur I *daven* to *Hashem* and beg Him to accept my *teshuvah*. I'm proud to be part of *klal Yisrael*. Just like Ruth said to Naomi: 'Your people are my people, your God is my God.'

"We live in confusing times. There are many things which make it hard to remain a strong Jew with *emunah* in *Hashem*. I want to thank my parents again for being the strong, understanding people they are. I thank *Hashem* every day for delivering me to such wonderful, special people. They have always tried to show me the right way, the Torah way. It's impossible for any of us to know what the future holds, but I would like to make one promise to my family: I will never forget who I am — a Jew, a *cheilek* of *klal Yisrael*, a part of the Jewish people."

EPILOGUE

ACH SUMMER, an international film festival is held in Jerusalem. Although we're not what you might call movie aficionados, we seem to have gotten on the organizers' mailing list and this year when the program arrived I noticed that "Dust in the Wind", a film from Taiwan, was scheduled to be screened. This film, I recalled, had received favorable critical attention. Set in rural Taiwan, it depicted the day-to-day activities of a single family against a backdrop of the anomalous relationship between Taiwan and Mainland China.

Rochel was enthusiastically in favor of our going to see it. "I think we should bring Devorah along," I said. "After all, it takes place in the country of her birth. I'd be very interested to see her reaction to it."

When I told Devorah later that we hoped she'd join us, she was decidedly cool to the idea, but since she had no other appointments or obligations for that time and sensed that it was something her parents very much wanted her to do, she grudgingly agreed. On the day of the showing we went together to the theater. We entered the auditorium and found our seats. Devorah sat between Rochel and me. As the lights dimmed, our anticipation grew.

In the opening scene an old Chinese woman walked slowly along a quiet, dusty village path calling for her

grandson, *"A chwei! A chwei!"* and suddenly I was trans-
posed. A flood of memories overwhelmed me. The folk melo-
dies accompanying the sound track, the images before my
eyes, the Chinese dialogue, pulled me back in time. The
effect was profound. Feelings and recollections long submerged mingled with the action on the screen. I was overcome; my eyes filled with tears. I looked over at Rochel. She
was crying softly. The two of us were lost in a nostalgic
reverie, until Devorah's voice broke through. "I don't believe
this, it's unreal! The movie is on for two seconds and you're
both crying your eyes out!"

Afterwards, driving home, I asked Devorah for her
impressions. "It was okay, I guess. A little slow-moving. At
one point I got mixed up and couldn't tell which character
was supposed to be the narrator." I waited for more, but she
had nothing to add.

Later that same evening, one of those rare moments
occurred when the boys were asleep and the house was filled
with the calm and peacefulness I usually associate only with
Shabbos. Rochel, Devorah and I were seated at the kitchen
table. "Devorah," I asked, "did you have any special feeling
when you saw the film?"

"Not really," she replied. "Was I supposed to?"

"Well, you know, it took place in Taiwan and some of the
people in the story were children your own age."

"Listen, Ta, I know you and Mom have this thing about
me feeling positive about Chinese people and Chinese culture, and I appreciate the things you've done since I was
small, like trying to help me remember my spoken Chinese,
and all the business with Chinese food, and Chinese music
and calligraphy. I want you to know that I'm not ashamed of
being born Chinese or looking Chinese — this was
Hashem's decision. But really, it just doesn't mean that
much to me. What really matters to me is that I'm Jewish."

For the second time that day, my eyes filled with tears.

ROCHEL'S POSTSCRIPT

MAZAL TOV! It's a boy!" Dr. Rosenberg announced triumphantly. It was June 28, 1985, the ninth of Tammuz, and I had just delivered our first "sabra", a mere seven minutes after entering Misgav Ladach Hospital [in Jerusalem]. This fourth, and by far the fastest of all my babies' births, had gone *so* quickly that Avraham was still outside parking the car when the baby decided to enter the world!

A moment later Avraham was at my side. With a proud glance at our new son, he smiled and asked how I was doing. *"I'm* fine, *baruch Hashem,"* I said, "but *poor* Devorah. She so much wanted a little sister!"

"Don't worry," Avraham replied with a confident nod. "You know Devorah. After the first three minutes of grumbling about *another* brother, she'll cuddle and care for that baby just as happily as she would have if it had been a girl."

I knew that my husband was right, and as he left to phone home and report the good news, I settled back and looked down at my newborn, already nursing contentedly. Just a dry diaper, some warm milk and an arm to snuggle into, and a tiny human being could be so satisfied. This moment of sharing with the child who for months had been a part of me, was the culmination of what seemed like a lifetime's odyssey

— a quest for something that had led us full circle to our roots, to *Hashem*, to Torah and *mitzvos*, to *Eretz Yisrael*. Now, ensconced in this quiet capsule of time, I understood what our Sages intended when they taught: "Wealthy is he who is happy with his lot." Gone was the desire or need to search, to travel, to wend our way through others' cultures and beliefs. We had, *baruch Hashem*, found our own.

Memories gently washed across the shores of my being — my childhood, enhanced by my parents' love and family's warmth; college, the beginning of independence and the place where I met my intended spouse; my first trip to Europe with my friend Irene, where at every American Express office in each city we visited I found one of "Allan's" letters waiting for me, wishing me back home; our marriage, and then graduate study at Cornell University, a year spiced with friends from the entire spectrum of the foreign student body; our teaching stint at the University of the West Indies on the islands of Trinidad and Tobago in the Caribbean, where the sun shimmered on the surface of deep blue waters and white sands all year 'round; our return to the United States, where I became involved in Special Education and the bitter-sweet work with children in need; and finally, our own futile attempts to start a family of our own.

I thought of myself crying in the darkness of my bedroom after meeting pregnant women on the street. I thought of the years of treatment for 'infertility', the charts, the pills, the strain on our marriage. And then, our decision to adopt, the resolution ours but the mode of execution surely that of a Higher Power.

A gift was bestowed on us that day in Taiwan, and it paved the way for an apparent *nes* in our time. It is, after all, not so uncommon for couples who adopt to soon afterwards have children of their own. But the conception of our first-born took place *four years after* Devorah's adoption, coinciding with her halachic conversion and our own conscious alteration of lifestyle and behavior, a fact which my dear friend and mentor, Rebbetzin Ruchoma Shain [*All For the Boss*], would call a "clear example of *hashgachah pratis.*"

Of course nothing occurs by accident. Hashem personally watches over and helps each individual and, ultimately, everything that happens is for the best. Through our ordeal we grew and matured. We gained insight and learned patience, which I, especially, had lacked in the early years of our marriage. Now, at the age of forty-one, I felt more equipped than ever before to re-assume the responsibilities of motherhood, and I felt happy within myself in that role.

Our children, at their tender ages, were already conquering *Chumash*, *Navi*, *Mishnah*, *Gemara*, the Hebrew language and more, all subjects with which we ourselves were still struggling. But as *ba'alei teshuvah*, there was something special we could give them: an appreciation of the beautiful world of *Yiddishkeit* and *frumkeit* into which they were born. We could teach them never to take it all for granted.

I sensed Avraham's presence in the room before I actually saw him standing by my side. "You were so deep in thought," he said softly, "I didn't want to disturb you."

"Just reminiscing," I replied. We both looked down at our little "sabra", who by now was sound asleep. Our eyes met, and without words or contact, everything essential was transmitted between us. It is said that in a good, solid marriage the Divine Presence rests between husband and wife, helping them along the way. In an atmosphere of *shalom bayis*, Hashem Himself dwells, creating the warmth and glow of a happy household. So I felt it to be with us, and I knew that we were blessed. With that glance that said all, I silently thanked God for this special partner to accompany me through life's difficulties and joys.

"By the way," I asked with a grin, "what did Devorah say?"

"Just what I had expected," Avraham answered. "At first she didn't believe that the baby had already been born. Then she said, with a mixture of hopefulness and resignation in her voice, 'Don't tell me, Ta — Ima had a boy!' There was about a five-second pause and then: 'Is he cute, Ta? Is Ima okay? When can I come to see them? Oh, gosh, another brother! Never mind, if you and Ima have three more sons, you can be assured a place in *Gan Eden*!''

We both laughed, and I thought to myself, not 'poor' Devorah by any means, but 'rich' in the true sense of the word. We all were, in fact — rich beyond our wildest dreams.

EIGHT DAYS LATER, Avraham spoke at the *bris* and his words expressed the pleasure and gratitude we all felt so deeply.

"The Matriarchs," he said, "knew that Yaakov would have twelve sons. That should have meant three sons for each of Jacob's four wives. When Leah gave birth to her fourth son, she gave special thanks because *Hashem* had given her more than her share. She named this son Yehudah, saying, הפעם אודה את ה' — 'Now I will praise *Hashem*.'

"Rochel and I waited twelve years before our first son was born, a gift from *Hashem*. Then we were blessed with a second son, and a third. Now, we have a fourth son, and we give special thanks because *Hashem* has given us much more than our share. Like Leah, we have named him Yehudah."

DEVORAH'S DIARY

January 18, 1983

Dear Diary,

What a trip! We're all exhausted. I thought we would never get here, and now that we're here, I'm not so sure we should have come! First, there was this mix-up with our tickets; because El Al is on strike, we had to fly Sabena. The El Al office in Miami was supposed to have had our tickets, but they didn't know anything about it. After my father made a bunch of frantic calls, the tickets arrived at Bubby's house by special delivery a few hours before our flight. We took a TWA flight from Miami to Kennedy Airport, and then a Sabena flight to Tel Aviv. TWA said that they wouldn't transfer our luggage to Sabena, but after my mother threw a hyper-fit, they finally did. I guess they felt sorry for us. We were supposed to have had a one-hour stop in Belgium which turned into a six-hour stop because of an air controllers' strike in Europe. Just our luck. We finally transferred to another Sabena airplane, a much smaller one with propellers. When we came into Ben Gurion airport there was a huge storm. My father was sitting next to the window over the wing, and it was hit by lightning! It was *really* scary.

There was a snow storm in Tel Aviv and Jerusalem when we arrived. They said it *never* snows in Israel. Ha! This was really quite unusual, people said. Right, well, unusual things always happen to me. When we landed, we found out that Sabena had left about half our luggage in Belgium. We had to spend another two hours at Ben Gurion before the Jewish Agency arranged transportation to the absorption center.

We arrived at midnight, after traveling something like twenty-six hours. The snow was really coming down. The absorption center in Gilo looked like something from outer space! There were these little tiny apartments that looked like cement boxes stacked one on top of another, all connected by outside staircases. You can imagine what it looked like. The driver from the Jewish Agency dumped our luggage on the street and took off. Gee, thanks, I thought.

We finally found the office. There was a young Russian guy on duty. When we told him our name, he said we weren't supposed to be there for another two days. Anyway, he found a key and helped bring our things up to our apartment. We had to climb about a thousand stairs in the snow to get there. The apartment had only two rooms and was freezing. I really felt like crying. Mom helped the smaller kids get into sleeping bags. They were so tired that they fell asleep immediately. The guy who brought us up to the apartment also gave us a tea kettle and some tea bags, so Mom made some tea for us. I really felt awful. I noticed a small note taped to the inside of the front door. It said, *"Beruchim Ha-ba'im* — Welcome to Israel!" Thanks.

February 2, 1983

Dear Diary,

I hate it here. I hate the absorption center and I hate my school. In other words, I'm miserable. I miss our old house and all my friends. I only understand about one-half or less of what is going on in my classes, and the teachers and other kids in my class are not all that friendly. My parents feel that I should try to stick it out, and that it's important for me to learn in Hebrew. I said that I'd try, but I don't know if I'll be able to make it....

February 10, 1983

Dear Diary,

Today our family was riding in a *sherut*. The driver noticed that my mother was holding the baby on her lap and that the baby wasn't too comfortable. He stopped the taxi and said he would get a pillow for the baby. My mother said it was okay, he didn't have to bother. He opened the trunk anyway, and took out a small pillow and gave it to her. He said, "He may be your son, but he is *our* child." Wasn't that nice?

February 15, 1983

Dear Diary,

I invited some of the kids in my class to visit me in Gilo, but they all said they were busy. There are hardly any religious kids in the *merkaz klitah*. It seems most of the new *olim* are from Argentina and Russia — with my Hebrew and their English we can really communicate. The religious *olim* from the United States are much younger than my parents, and have small children much younger than me. It's great for babysitting! I did make one friend, Sarah Bass. She lives in the neighborhood. Her family made *aliyah* about four years ago and she's been helping me a lot.

March 14, 1983

Dear Diary,

Came into my class and someone had written "Goy" again on my desk.

May 16, 1983

Dear Diary,

Today I went shopping in the shuk for cucumbers. I was standing right next to this butcher's stall with a lot of dead chickens hanging by their feet. There was a young woman who asked for some meat. After the butcher started to weigh it out on the scale, she told him it was too much. The butcher took a few slices off. The lady said it was still too much. The butcher began to get annoyed and said in a gruff voice, "Don't you feed your husband?" The lady began to cry. The butcher asked her why she was crying and she said, "I don't have a husband, he was killed in Lebanon." Then the butcher began to cry and went into the back room. His partner came over and explained that he had just lost his wife. I felt really bad for both of them.

July 19, 1983

Dear Diary,

I'm feeling really awful. I want to go back. Today was *Tisha Be-Av*, and at the *Kosel*, when I was *davening*, this lady started to scream at me, "You don't belong here! You're not really Jewish, what are you doing here praying?" I was really hurt and embarrassed. The worst part was that no one did anything to stop her or talk to her. I was separated from Mom, and I just felt like crying. People are always bothering me.

September 13, 1983

Dear Diary,

Today Devorah Gottlieb and I went to *shlug kaparos* in Meah Shearim. It was the weirdest experience. The chickens were *live*. This man *shlugged* it around my head for me because I wouldn't touch it. Devorah was laughing her head off. Just as the man was swinging it around my head for the last time, I heard these two small kids talking to each other. One asked the other in a puzzled voice, "What, they *shlug kaparos* in China too?"

April 13, 1984

Dear Diary,

I just want to go back to America, where being Chinese isn't a novelty — like, people don't come up to you asking dumb questions. Okay, maybe people are curious, but it's very annoying to be asked the same questions every day. Like, "Are you Chinese?" Not even polite, like, "Excuse me, but are you Chinese?" If the questions were asked politely maybe I wouldn't mind so much. But it makes me feel like a nothing. They get their answer and then they leave. "Are you Jewish?" is another question they ask. So I answer. Other people, of course, get more personal, and just don't go away. I've learned a lot about answering questions, like when people ask "Where are you from?" I answer "America," because they didn't ask where I was *born*, did they? That answer gives them something to think about.

Baruch Hashem, I've got great friends. They stick with me through thick and thin. They stick up for me and are always by my side. And they cheer me up when I'm down — and persuade me I'm normal and not some circus freak. I don't know how I would survive without them! It's very hard — people say I'll get through it! Ha, that's funny.

April 15, 1984

Dear Diary,

There are some *weird* people in this world! This man came up to me and just started telling me his whole life story. Let me tell you, it was one weird experience! He saw I was Chinese and started off on his "adventures" in China. I said something like "Oh, very interesting, but I gotta go — 'bye!" And then he started gibbering in Chinese. I don't even understand Chinese.

April 24, 1984

Dear Diary,

There are some nice, normal, people in this world too. Last night this man came up and asked me very nicely and politely where something was. So I took him there. On the way, he asked very nicely, with an "Excuse me for asking, but..." and the usual question, "Are you Chinese?" Then he said, "Really, pardon me for asking, but are you Jewish?" After I answered, he got so embarrassed. He started apologizing! I said it was okay because everyone asks, but he kept on saying he was sorry. I felt so bad for him. He was really embarrassed; I had to reassure him a million times it was okay. It gave me such a nice feeling, though. Because you can be polite and curious, and you can be rude and curious. And it was so nice to be treated like a person, not just an answering machine.

June 4, 1984

Dear Diary,

Tonight Chaviva Saslow's sister had a *bas mitzvah* party and I got my first marriage proposal! It was a rainy night so I took a taxi from Bayit Vegan (the neighborhood where we live now). On the way there, I had a very interesting conversation with the taxi driver. He asked all the usual questions, and then we got into a discussion about *yiddishkeit* and on being *frum*. All of a sudden he said, "Listen, if I become *frum* — will you marry me?" I said, "What?" thinking maybe I heard him wrong — my Hebrew isn't the greatest. I asked him to repeat what he just said. So he repeated it, and I was right! So I said, "Well, um, I'd like for you to become *frum* and everything, but I'm not going to marry you!" And he said, "Please, listen, I'll go to that *ba'al teshuvah* yeshiva, and learn and wear a yarmulka — will you marry me?" So I said, "Well, um, please go to yeshiva and learn, and become *frum*, but I'm *not* going to marry you."

Baruch Hashem we finally reached the hotel where Chaviva's sister was having her *bas mitzvah*. I paid him, said thank you and wished him luck. He said thanks, and said maybe he'd see me around Bayit Vegan some day. I sure hope not!

July 1, 1984

Dear Diary,

Today, when I was walking back from the *makolet* with Sara Katz, these boys started up. Sara started yelling back, "Leave her alone — stop calling her names!" I was so surprised. I've learned to ignore it already, and I sort of block it out now when I hear it. But there was Sara, just yelling away, sticking up for me. It made me feel really good.

Motza'ei Shabbos,
October 20, 1984

Dear Diary,

I don't want people to walk around on their tiptoes, scared of mentioning anything about China or the Chinese. Like last night at Yudit's house. Her aunt came to visit from America, and Yudit's sister, Shoshana, dropped all the silverware she was drying. "Great, Shana," Yudit's aunt said. "You know in China..." she began, and then gasped and covered her mouth. It took me a minute to realize she was embarrassed because I was there. So I left, but I was really dying to know the end of the joke. So the next day, today, I asked Yudit how it went. She couldn't remember, so she asked her aunt. It's not even so funny, but here it is: How do the people in China name their kids? They drop the silverware, and whatever sound comes out, that's what their kid is called!

November 4, 1984

Dear Diary,

I really got angry today. Usually I can keep calm even if I'm burning up inside, but today I exploded. I was riding the No. 21 bus from the central bus station back to Bayit Vegan. There were these three kids, they looked about fourteen or fifteen years old, and they were making dumb remarks about this Ethiopian girl who was about my age. They were talking very loudly and calling her all sorts of bad names and laughing about it.

Well, it really got me mad. I'm sort of used to it but I figured this girl just arrived in Israel and this was no way to treat a newcomer! So I just marched up to these kids — there were two boys and a girl. I started yelling at them in Hebrew — which was funny in itself — and told them that we had as much right to be in Israel as they did; that I might be from China, and this girl might be from Africa, but that Israel was just as much our home as it was theirs! And if they ever took the time to look in the *Chumash*, it says in *Parshas Mishpatim* in *Sefer Shemos*, "Do not hurt the feelings of a foreigner," which Rashi says means anyone from another country, "because we were foreigners in Egypt." They were so surprised that a Chinese girl opened her mouth, with Hebrew words coming out, or maybe my words had some effect on them. Whatever, they kept quiet for the rest of the bus trip. Eppie, my very good friend who was with me, was really proud I did that.

May 20, 1985

Dear Diary,

Today coming home from school, these boys started up again, the same boys who kicked me yesterday. But this time they got very violent. They threw a raw egg at me, but I ducked, and instead it hit Chaviva Saslow who was right behind me! Shifra Kubie laughed nervously. I felt *awful*! Because of me, Chaviva was a mess — egg dripping down her head, onto her coat, down her chin. If she hadn't been with me, it never would have happened to her. She's really a great friend — she tried to make me feel better by cracking a joke about it. "Well, it says in all the beauty magazines that raw egg is good for your hair." We all laughed feebly. We ran back to the school building, but no one was there who could do anything. So we took a bus to the central bus station — a total waste of money because it's only one bus stop. On the bus, everyone was staring at Chaviva like she was weird. Shifra and I wiped her with a bunch of tissues.

Motza'ei Shavuos, 1985

Dear Diary,

Miriam and Numie came to pick me up at a quarter past three this morning to walk to the *Kosel*. We started to walk toward Michlalah [College for Women]. By the time we got to Michlalah, we were twenty-five girls! As we walked down the steep sides of the valley there were about fifty of us, and the crowd kept on growing all along the way. It was really nice. As we walked through the Arab shuk we must've been thousands of Jews walking together! It was really something. When we came to the *Kosel* there were people everywhere. Since it wasn't time to *daven* yet, many of the yeshiva *bachurim* started to sing and dance in a huge circle. It was beautiful. As I was *davening shacharis*, the morning light grew brighter. The stones of the *Kosel* seemed to glow. This was the day *Hashem* gave us the Torah. I felt so proud to be part of *klal Yisrael*.

March 13, 1986

Dear Diary,

Because Numie's parents were in England and I was staying with her in her empty apartment, she asked me to come along with her when she visited her grandparents, Rabbi and Mrs. Silver, on Michlin Street. She wanted to borrow her grandmother's blowdryer. I'm pretty close with her grandparents so of course I said okay. I was in their kitchen helping with the dishes when the doorbell rang, and Numie's grandmother asked me to please get the door. I opened it, and there were these two Sephardi *bachurim*. They seemed a *little* surprised to see me. "*Tzedakah*," they said. "Okay, please wait a minute," I answered. I went back and told the Silvers and Rabbi Silver gave me some money to give to the boys. They said, "Thank you," and left.

About twenty minutes later, Numie and I left the Silvers and walked over to Numie's house around the corner on Uziel Street. We had only been in the apartment for about five minutes when the doorbell rang. I was closest to the door so I answered it. It was the same two Sephardi *bachurim*! When they saw me their eyes seemed to widen but all they said was *"Tzedakah."* "Okay," I said, "wait a sec." I called to Numie, and she told me to take some money from the breakfront and give it to them. They said, "Thank you," and left.

About ten minutes later I told Numie I was going back to my house to get my stuff. I walked down the street to my apartment. Soon after I arrived, the doorbell rang. Guess what! It was the *same two* Sephardi *bachurim*! Their eyes were *really* wide open this time, and their mouths seemed to drop a bit, but all they said was *"Tzedakah."* So I went to my bag and gave them two shekels. This time they didn't even say thank you; they were probably too shocked! While they were walking away I saw them shaking their heads. They probably never saw a Chinese person before! And now they saw *three* (or one, however you look at it). They probably thought I was triplets.

May 10, 1986

Dear Diary,

It was so embarrassing! I went with my family to this Glatt Kosher Chinese restaurant last night. The food was pretty good. I needed the bathroom, so I got up from the table. On my way back, some man motioned me over to his table. As I approached he gave me his bill and a bunch of shekels. I thought, great! money — but why? Finally, I realized what he thought. I had to explain that I was *not* a waitress. But I paid his bill for him anyway.

September 1, 1986

Dear Diary,

Today I was an absolute wreck. I started my first day in what is known officially as the Beth Jacob Teachers Institute, Jerusalem; unofficially — Bais Ya'akov High.

I was really nervous because there are so many girls! I didn't know a single soul, and I felt tiny in the huge crowd. Finally, I caught sight of some girls I knew slightly from Bayit Vegan. They motioned me over to join them. I was very grateful, because at least now I had someone to cling to. I mean, I could only stare at my watch for a certain amount of time, right? Man, was I getting stares!!! I was *super* nervous about how I'd be accepted.

There were about a thousand girls packed into the auditorium. We were all waiting to hear our names called and get divided into classes. My friends' names were called, but not mine! I was in a panic. Finally, only I was left in the auditorium. The lady who called the names was just about to come and ask me where I belonged, when my friend Bracha Pollack came running in. She told me that the teacher in our class was calling the roll, and my name was on it! In the confusion of dividing the girls, my name was omitted from the master list. What a relief!

I thanked *Hashem* gratefully in my heart for putting me with my friends.

When I entered the classroom, I braced myself for the stares and questions. But — there were no stares and no questions!! I was accepted into the *chevrah* as one of the girls. And so begins my new school year.

October 13, 1986

Dear Diary,

School is very hard. The language is really a problem. Sometimes I just feel like giving up. But Tobi Friedlander who lives in Geula, my very good American friend in school, always helps me before my tests. She studies with me, and translates the test for me, which takes away some of *her* test time. I could never get through the tests without her.

October 29, 1986

Dear Diary,

The funniest thing happened today. Miriam Geisler and I were on the bus, returning from a *Simchas Beis Ha-shoevah*. We were sitting across from three *chassidishe* boys about six years old. They were talking to each other, when one glanced (as usual) at us — and started staring in shock. One of the others turned to see what his friend was staring at — then we had *two chassidishe* boys staring at us in shock. *Then*, when the third boy noticed his friends weren't listening to him and that he was talking to himself, we had all *three chassidishe* boys staring at us in shock. One boy asked the other: "Hey, Meyer — she's Chinese?" His friend started to answer, "No," but just at that moment Miriam said softly to me, but not softly enough because they heard, "She's Jewish, you nerds," and he continued with, "No, she's Jewish." The third boy said, "She's Sephardi." The second boy said, "Maybe she's Ashkenazi (which I am) but the third one said, "No, can't you tell? She's a Chinese Jewish Sephardi!" So it was then that Miriam and I let go and *plotzed*, but the boys couldn't see what was so funny. So now I am officially a Chinese Sephardi Jew!!

Motza'ei Shabbos,
January 3, 1987

Dear Diary,

This past Shabbos my class went to Bnei Brak. Amazing
— the food was even edible!!! There was a real feeling of
achdus throughout the *Shabbaton*, and I really felt a part of
it. It was such a nice, warm feeling to know I "belonged".

February 9, 1987

Dear Diary,

The most embarrassing things happen to me! As my
friend Eppie says — I get myself into some pretty unusual
situations! I wanted to buy some needles in Meah Shearim.
So I went into a store and asked for *machatonim*. In
Hebrew, needles are *machatim* so I got confused. The store-
keeper looked at me like I was crazy. He asked me to repeat
myself. *"Machatonim,"* I said. "Listen," he said, "you want
machatonim, you got the wrong place! What do you think I
am — a *shadchan*? You want *machatonim*, go upstairs to
Mrs. Segal, *she's* a *shadchanta*." I thought, "Huh? I don't
need a *shadchan*, I need needles!" So I told him I saw them
in the window. The man for *sure* must've thought I was
crazy. "You saw *machatonim* in the window? Show me," he
said, walking to the window. I pointed. "Oh," he said, *"machatim*! Why didn't you *say* so?"

May 18, 1987

Dear Diary,

Today, on the way home from school, I took the 39 bus to Bayit Vegan with Bracha Pollack. Boy was it crowded. I just managed to get on and wedge myself between the door and the little space around the driver. I couldn't move left or right, up or down. Just my luck, I get a driver who is fascinated by Orientals. As usual, he takes me for Japanese. *"Yapanit,"* he says to me. I go into my protective routine for such events — *ignore*!, *look away*! This time I couldn't use technique no. 3, *move away*! because I couldn't move at all, not even an inch. So far nothing unusual, just normal curiosity and stupid questions and comments.

Then this driver starts to serenade me and he starts singing opera! I didn't recognize any of it. For all I know it could have been Mozart, Verdi, Puccini. Anyway, whatever it was, it was awful. If I could have made a hole in the bus and dropped through it, I would have. Bracha was hysterical with laughter. I could see my friends and people from the neighborhood looking up to see what was going on. Boy, was I embarrassed!

Finally, after what seemed like hours, we arrived at my stop. I was boiling. Usually I don't say anything but this time as I got off I told him in a haughty voice, "For your information, I'm Chinese, not Japanese." But it didn't even work because he didn't hear me! So as I was walking down Ha-pisgah Street, he drove the bus slowly after me, and shouted through the open door, "What? What did you say?" which only made it more embarrassing. Imagine having a *bus* follow you down the street! After a few seconds he gave up. Which just goes to show, it doesn't pay to open your mouth!

P.S. Tonight my father told me that Mr. Goldstein, who is in his *daf yomi shiur*, came up and told him that he was on the same bus with me and saw the episode of the singing driver. My father said that at the last stop when everyone got off and the driver was alone, Mr. Goldstein went up to the driver. He told the driver that I lived in the neighborhood, that I was a very special person and he knew that I became embarrassed and upset when people did things that made me stand out in public. The driver said, "Really, I didn't know. Tell her I'm very sorry." That was really nice of Mr. Goldstein. I feel better. Maybe I should try to learn something about opera.

August 24, 1987

Dear Diary

GUESS WHAT?! My very, very best friend — that's right, Eppie Toledano — became a *kallah*! I'm so excited! Of course, *I* knew from the beginning they would marry each other — it just took a while for *them* to figure it out!!

His name is James Lasry and he's twenty. The *vort* was August 23rd. It was beautiful, and Eppie looked stunning. The whole time we were hugging and grinning at each other.

I'm so hyped up I can't write anymore!

August 25, 1987

Dear Diary,

Now that I'm calmer, I have so much to write! I'm so excited I could tell the whole world! I've known the engagement was unofficial for the past two months. And me with my big mouth had a problem keeping it shut. So after eight weeks and six days of being quiet, I exploded! I called the whole world!

It's kinda scary, because it means we're all getting older. I mean, we're not little kids anymore. We're growing up. It feels strange that your best friend — the kid who got into so much trouble with you, the kid who stayed up all night laughing with you, the kid who did *everything* with you — is getting married. You know what I mean?

Anyway, I wish her and Jamie a healthy, happy marriage, filled with much *nachas* and lotsa children, who should grow up to be true *Bnei Torah* and *Bnos Yisrael*.

August 26, 1987

Dear Diary,

I'm really disgusted. The way people simply talk just to talk. It really upsets me a lot. If you run out of topics of conversation, discuss Torah!

The reason I'm so upset is that people in Bayit Vegan are talking about Eppie — that she's so crazy getting engaged at sixteen and by the time she gets married — אי"ה, Novembeer 29th — she'll only be sixteen-and-a-half. I'm so sick about it because Eppie is really upset. I've known since the day she got engaged that this is what people were saying. But I wasn't going to tell her! I knew it would hurt her so much.

I mean, it's different when people say that I was found in a garbage can, or left gift-wrapped in front of my parents' house, or found on an archeological dig by my father — who's a sociologist, not an archeologist! (And thanks, that means I'm really five thousand years old! I just *look* like I'm fifteen-and-a-half.) Or that I was lying in front of an oncoming train on the tracks, and my father leaped down and saved me. (My father likes that story the best.) I mean, those are *funny*! Well, *now* I think so, but when I first heard them, believe me I didn't think so. I was very hurt. Oh, wait

— I left out the one that I was living with Christian missionaries (my parents) and *nebach*, they were trying to re-convert me!

But it really upsets me the way people just gossip. It causes much more damage than they know.

November 8, 1987

Dear Diary,

Tonight, right before my seven-year-old brother Dahveed was falling asleep, we were having the funniest conversation! He said to me: "Devorah, where's your real mommy?"

So I said, "I don't know."

Dahveed: "You really don't know?"

Me: "Really."

Dahveed: "My mommy is your mommy now, right?"

Me: "Right."

Dahveed: "Your real mommy probably didn't have enough money to keep you."

Me: "Maybe."

Dahveed: "Right you were found on a bench in a train station?"

Me: "Right."

Dahveed: "You know how I know?"

Me: "How?"

Dahveed: "My friend told me!"

November 18, 1987

Dear Diary,

Today a very good and close friend told me that she was asked by another person why I don't have plastic surgery. So this friend asked me. I know the question wasn't meant to hurt me or anything, because we're good friends and discuss anything. It was just out of curiosity. So I answered that אי"ה when I get married and have kids, they'll all come out looking Chinese! This friend said it's not necessarily true, and she's right because I know a girl whose mother is Japanese and you would never know! Besides, who'd want a doctor fooling around with your eyes? But the most important reason is because *Hashem* made me the way I am — who am I to decide my physical appearance? ב"ה I'm healthy and I look normal, so really, why should I change? This is the way *Hashem* made me, so this is the way I'll stay!

GLOSSARY

Glossary

The following glossary provides a partial explanation of some of the
Hebrew and Yiddish (Y.) words and phrases used in this book. The
spelling and explanations reflect the way the specific word is used
herein. Often, there are alternate spellings and meanings for the
words. Foreign words and phrases which are immediately followed by
a translation in the text are not included in this section.

ACHDUS: unity.
ALEF BEIS: the Hebrew alphabet.
ALIYAH: lit., ascent; immigration to Israel.

BA'AL TESHUVAH: a penitent; a Jew who has become Orthodox or
   returned to observant Judaism.
BACHUR(IM): lit., a Jewish youth; a YESHIVAH student.
BAR MITZVAH: a Jewish male who reaches the age of thirteen,
   whereupon he becomes halachically responsible for his actions
   and obligated to fulfill the MITZVOS as an adult; the celebration
   of this occasion.
BARUCH HASHEM: "thank God."
BAS MITZVAH: a Jewish female who reaches the age of twelve,
   whereupon she becomes halachically responsible for her
   actions and obligated to fulfill the MITZVOS as an adult; the
   celebration of this occasion.
BECHOR: a firstborn son.
BEIS DIN: a Jewish court of law.
BENTCH: (Y.) to bless.
BERACHAH: a blessing.
BERAISA: a passage of the Talmud written by Jewish scholars of the
   first and second centuries C.E.
BIMAH: lit., platform or dais; the raised platform from which the
   Torah is read in the synagogue.
BITACHON: lit., security; faith in Divine Providence.
BNEI TORAH: lit., sons of Torah; learned, observant Jews.
BNOS YISRAEL: lit., daughters of Israel; observant Jewish girls.
BRIS MILAH: the rite of circumcision.

CHAG SAMEACH: "happy holiday."

CHALLOS: (pl.) special loaves of bread (usually braided) eaten on the Sabbath and Festivals.

CHASSIDISHE: (Y.) Hassidic.

CHAVRUSA: a study partner.

CHAZAL: acronym meaning "our Sages, of blessed memory."

CHAZAN: the leader of the prayer services in the synagogue.

CHESSED: kindness.

CHEVRAH: society.

CHINUCH: Jewish education.

CHOZRIM BE-TESHUVAH: (pl.) those who have returned to observant Judaism.

CHUMASH: the Pentateuch.

DAF YOMI SHIUR: a lesson in *daf yomi* — the worldwide synchronized study of one page of Talmud per day. (The entire Talmud is completed every seven years.)

DAVEN: (Y.) to pray.

DAVKA: (colloq.) contrarily; for the sake of being contrary or spiteful.

DERECH: path; way.

DVAR TORAH: lit., a word of Torah; an oration based on a Torah passage or verse and various commentaries thereon.

EICHAH: the Book of Lamentations.

EMUNAH: faith.

ERETZ YISRAEL: the Land of Israel.

EREV: eve.

FRUM: (Y.) religious.

FRUMKEIT: (Y.) religiosity.

GAN EDEN: lit., the Garden of Eden; the World to Come.

GEMARA: commentary on the MISHNAH; a volume of the Talmud.

GOY: (Y.) a gentile.

HAFTARAH: a relevant chapter of the Prophets read each Sabbath and Festival following the Torah reading.

HAKADOSH BARUCH HU: "the Holy One, blessed be He."

HALACHAH: the body of Jewish law based on the Torah which determines normative Orthodox behavior.

HASHEM YISBARACH: "God, may He be blessed."

HATZLACHAH: success.

KALLAH: a bride.

KASHER: (Y.) to render "kosher", *i.e.*, to make suitable in accordance with Jewish dietary laws.

KASHRUS: Jewish dietary laws.

KESHER: bond.

KIDDUSH: benediction recited over wine on the Sabbath and Jewish holidays.

KIPPOT: yarmulkas.

KLAL YISRAEL: all of Jewry.

KOHAIN: a descendant of the priestly family of Aaron.

KOL ISHA: lit., a woman's voice; the prohibition for a man to hear a woman singing.

KOSEL: the Western Wall of the Holy Temple.

MACHAT(IM): needle.

MACHATONIM: (Y.) (pl.) in-laws.

MAGGID...SHIUR: the teacher of a Jewish study group.

MAKOLET: neighborhood grocery store.

MATZOS: the unleavened bread eaten by Jews on Passover.

MAZAL: fortune.

MAZAL TOV: lit., good fortune; congratulations.

MEGILLAS ESTHER: the Scroll of Esther.

MERKAZ KLITAH: an absorption center for new Israeli immigrants.

METAPELET: governess; babysitter.

MIDRASH RABBAH: a compilation of interpretations of Scripture and parables by the authors of the Talmud.

MIKVEH: a ritual bath.

MISHLEI: the Book of Proverbs.

MISHNAH: the primary compilation of the Oral Law first written down in the late second century C.E. (The MISHNAH and the GEMARA comprise the Talmud.)

MITZVOS: (pl.) Torah commandments.

MOHEL: a Jewish ritual circumcisor.

MORAH: (f.) a teacher.

MOSHAV: an Israeli commune.

MOTZA'EI SHABBOS: Saturday evening after the conclusion of the Sabbath.

MOTZA'EI SHAVUOS: the evening after the conclusion of the Pentacost Festival.

NACHAS: (Y.) pleasure.

NAVI: the Books of the Prophets.

NEBACH: (Y.) unfortunately.

NES: a miracle.

OLIM: (pl.) immigrants to Israel.

PARSHAS MISHPATIM: one of the weekly Torah readings including Exodus 21-24.

PASUK: a Torah verse.

PESACH: Passover.

PIDYON HA-BEN: redemption of the firstborn son; the celebration of this occasion.

PLOTZ: (Y.) (colloq.) collapse from laughter or embarrassment.

POSEKIM: (pl.) rabbinic authoritiies who decide questions of HALACHAH.

PSAK: a halachic decision.

PURIM: the Jewish Festival of Lots.

RAV: rabbi.

REBBE(IM): (Y.) rabbi and teacher.

REBBETZIN: (Y.) the wife of a rabbi.

ROSH HASHANAH: the Jewish new year.

ROSH YESHIVAH: the dean of a Torah academy.

SANDAK: the man honored with holding the infant, the highest honor at a BRIS MILAH.

SEFER: a sacred book or scroll.

SEFER TORAH: a scroll of the Torah.

SEUDAS MITZVAH: the festive meal in celebration of the observance of a MITZVAH, e.g., wedding, BAR MITZVAH, etc.

SHABBATON: a weekend get-together devoted to spiritual inspiration.

SHABBOS: the Sabbath.

SHACHARIS: the morning prayer service.

SHADCHAN(TA): a matchmaker (Y. — f.).

SHALOM BAYIS: marital tranquility.

SHALOM ZACHAR: a festive celebration on the first Friday evening after the birth of a boy.

SHERUT: lit., service; an intercity shuttle taxi.

SHOFAR: a ram's horn sounded during the High Holidays services.

SHLITA: acronym meaning "may he live a good, long life, amen."

SHLUG KAPAROS: (Y.) (colloq.) the symbolic transfer of the punishment for one's sins to a live chicken on the eve of Yom Kippur, followed by the giving of charity.

SHOMREI MITZVOS: (pl.) observers of MITZVOS; Orthodox Jews.

SIDDUR: the Jewish prayerbook.

SIMCHAH: lit., joy; a joyous celebration.

SIMCHAS BEIS HA-SHOEVA: lit., the rejoicing in the water sources; a nightly musical celebration observed during the intermediate days of SUKKOS in reminiscence of such celebration in the Holy Temple.

SUKKAH: a thatched hut constructed for and in which Orthodox Jews dwell during SUKKOS.

SUKKOS: the Festival of the Tabernacles.

TALMID(IM): a Torah student.

TALLIT: a prayer shawl.

TANACH: acronym meaning the Pentateuch, the Prophets and the Writings, which together comprise the twenty-four books of the Jewish Bible.

TEFILLIN: two black leather boxes containing Torah verses which are bound to the arm and head of adult males during morning prayers.

TESHUVAH: penitence.

TISHA BE-AV: the Ninth of Av; the day (in the Hebrew calendar) of fasting and mourning in remembrance of the destruction of the Holy Temples.

TREIF: (Y.) (colloq.) unfit for consumption or use by Orthodox Jews.

TZEDAKAH: alms.

TZITZIS: lit., fringe; a four-cornered fringed garment worn by Orthodox Jewish males, usually under their shirts.

VORT: (Y.) lit., word; festive meal at which the groom promises (gives his word) to wed the bride.

YAHRTZEIT: (Y.) anniversary of a death.

YAPANIT: (f.) a Japanese.

YESHIVAH: a Torah academy.

YICHUD: seclusion.

YIDDISHKEIT: (Y.) Judaism.

YOM TOV: a Jewish holiday.